Notable Figures in Canadian History

Unveiling the Extraordinary Lives and Impact of Canada's Most Prominent Historical Icons

Welcome Aboard, Check Out This Limited-Time Free Bonus!

Ahoy, reader! Welcome to the Ahoy Publications family, and thanks for snagging a copy of this book! Since you've chosen to join us on this journey, we'd like to offer you something special.

Check out the link below for a FREE e-book filled with delightful facts about American History.

But that's not all - you'll also have access to our exclusive email list with even more free e-books and insider knowledge. Well, what are ye waiting for? Click the link below to join and set sail toward exciting adventures in American History.

Access your bonus here

https://ahoypublications.com/

Or, Scan the QR code!

Table of Contents

Introduction

Canada is a well-developed, first-world country today, but just over 150 years ago, it didn't even exist (as a nation). How did it become one of the most advanced countries in the world from nothing in such a short span of time? It was due to the efforts of a select few individuals throughout history who molded it into a formidable nation.

This book will unfold the spectacular lives of these exceptional individuals, from their astounding feats to their eccentric personalities. How did they manage to transform a nation that stretches over four million square miles? What made them uniquely qualified to do so? What hardships did they face and overcome (or failed to do so) during their journey?

There was the founder of Canada, a man with a unique vision who also had the courage to follow through on his dreams. His inspirational speeches still echo across the land today. Before him came a peculiar explorer who, along with his group of Indigenous peoples, led daring expeditions into the far north beyond the Arctic Circle in an attempt to expand the country's borders and human knowledge.

A great nation was founded and expanded but was yet to be nurtured. As wars raged across Canada and beyond, many heroes emerged with their efforts to bring peace, some through political means while others through more violence. Amid those battles and political machinations arose a man whose name would be etched in historical records forever, thanks to his extraordinary invention that is still in use today.

The 20th century not only brought World War I to Canada's gates but also great progress, primarily due to one man who would go on to become one of the finest prime ministers in the country's history. However, it's the women who would eventually make an even more significant impact on the Canadian landscape.

Two female leaders fought for equal rights back when it was a White man's world. One author, in particular, took literature to newer heights with her intricate prose and mesmerizing word-building skills.

This book narrates all these stories – and more – in vivid detail. The rich and complex Canadian history will come alive in these pages like in no other book. Its richness is made even richer, and its complexity has been simplified so that children and adults will both enjoy the fascinating tales. Everything regarding the notable figures of the country is explained thoroughly with clear illustrations wherever necessary so that the reader won't need to Google for more information at all!

Chapter 1: Sir John A. Macdonald and the Birth of Canada

Any book on Canadian history is incomplete without the remarkable achievements of Sir John A. Macdonald. He was responsible for merging three large North American provinces together to form one great nation. He was one of the most important "Fathers of Confederation" who gave birth to Canada.

John A. Macdonald.
https://commons.wikimedia.org/wiki/File:Portrait_of_John_A_Macdonald_by_Delos_C_Bell.jpg

Looking at Canada on the world map, it's easy to mistake it for a nation that has been around for a thousand years. It consists of one great landmass with a collection of smaller islands around. If at all, one might say that the islands were initially separate, but the large landmass was always Canada. However, it didn't even exist as a country over 160 years ago.

It was scattered rubble of different colonies and provinces with no cohesive and competitive governance. A group of like-minded visionaries created a formidable nation under strong rule from the rubble. One person contributed more than most, and despite his flaws, he is still hailed as one of the most influential figures in Canadian history.

Biography

Born on January 11, 1815, in Glasgow, Scotland, John Alexander Macdonald was the third child in a family of five sons and one daughter. His father, Hugh Macdonald, was a mildly successful merchant who fell on hard times and eventually became bankrupt. In 1820, the family immigrated to Canada, settling in Kingston, Upper Canada (now Ontario), in search of better prospects.

Life in Upper Canada in the early 19th century was challenging, marked by economic uncertainty and social upheaval. Hugh tried his hand at managing shops in the challenging environment but faced a string of failures. Thus, John grew up in a household with limited means.

Despite the hardships, young John showed promise from an early age. He attended local schools in Kingston, where he received a basic education that would serve as the foundation for his later intellectual pursuits. Around 1825, his family's financial condition improved slightly, so he was sent to a more affluent secondary school in Kingston.

Five years later, he would have gone on to study literature had his family been well off, but due to their increasing financial problems (his father was struggling to work as a local magistrate), he left formal education at the age of 15 and began working as a clerk in a local law office.

Apart from literature, John eventually developed a passion for history and political theory. In his free time, he devoured books about the history of British rule in North America and became well-versed in the common political tactics used at the time.

John regretted his decision to leave school so soon, but he always respected and loved his family, never blaming them for his mistakes.

This can be seen when he named one of his own sons after his father, Hugh John Macdonald.

During his tenure as a clerk, John's parents decided he should become a lawyer. It turned out to be the right decision for him since he showed immediate aptitude and affinity for the profession. Back then, there were no law schools or a structured study regime for becoming a lawyer. Aspirants had to pass an examination set by *"The Law Society of Upper Canada,"* apprentice for a reputable lawyer, and take another examination to test what they learned.

Macdonald traveled to York (Toronto) for the first examination, which he easily passed. Then, he studied the profession under the guidance of George Mackenzie, a prominent Kingston lawyer. Mackenzie died of cholera during the apprenticeship, so Macdonald returned to Kingston in 1835, where he began his own practice. Though he wasn't qualified or experienced as a lawyer, he managed to land a few good clients.

A year later, he was called to the Bar (a legal term for being qualified as a lawyer) at the age of 21. Macdonald quickly established himself as a skilled lawyer known for his sharp intellect and persuasive courtroom tactics. According to Richard Gwyn, one of his biographers, "As a criminal lawyer who took on dramatic cases, Macdonald got himself noticed well beyond the narrow confines of the Kingston business community. He was operating now in the arena where he would spend by far the greatest part of his life - the court of public opinion."

In 1837, like every other man between the ages of 18 and 60, he was called to fight alongside the British against the rebellions of the Hunters' Lodges, a secret society of Lower Canadian refugees. He carried a musket and marched from place to place but never got the chance to fire it.

Macdonald recalled one of his marches to Toronto while conversing with his secretary after the rebellions, *"The day was hot, my feet were blistered — I was but a weary boy — and I thought I should have dropped under the weight of the old flint musket which galled my shoulder. But I managed to keep up with my companion, a grim old soldier who seemed impervious to fatigue."*

He reached the pinnacle of his legal career in the early 1840s when he made a lot of money and invested in real estate throughout Toronto. However, his personal life was in shambles. His father died in 1841, and he began suffering from an unknown illness. To recover from his emotional and physical turmoil, he took a vacation to Britain, where he met his first cousin, Isabella Clark.

The two immediately hit it off, and soon after Macdonald returned to Kingston, Isabella followed. They got married in 1843. They had one child together, a daughter named Mary, who sadly died in infancy. Despite personal tragedies and professional challenges, Macdonald's legal career flourished, and he soon became involved in local politics.

Isabella Clark.
https://commons.wikimedia.org/wiki/File:Isabella_Clark.jpg

His entry into politics came at a time of great change in Canada. The Union Act of 1840 merged Upper and Lower Canada into the United Province of Canada, and political tensions between English-speaking populations were high. Macdonald aligned himself with the Conservative Party, which advocated maintaining strong ties with Britain and resisting the influence of French Canadian nationalists.

In 1844, he was elected to the Kingston City Council, marking the beginning of his political career. He quickly rose through the ranks of the Conservative Party, gaining a reputation as a shrewd strategist and effective communicator.

His Early Political Career

John's rise within the Conservative Party was swift, but he underwent several ups and downs in his personal life. His wife, Isabella, began suffering from a recurring illness soon after his selection to the Kingston City Council. Hoping that a change of climate might improve her health,

John took her to Savannah, Georgia, in the U.S. Her condition didn't improve much, but by 1847, the couple had something to cheer for – a healthy little boy they named John A. Macdonald Jr.

Thus, from 1844 to 1847, Macdonald often traveled to Savannah, but his absences and personal problems miraculously didn't affect his political career. In his own words, *"Politics is a game requiring great coolness and an utter abnegation of prejudice and personal feeling."*

Instead, he gained several promotions. In 1846, he was conferred the title "Queen's Counsel," a prestigious honor in the British monarchy. He was also offered a job assisting the Minister of Justice, but since he had already found his passion in politics, he declined the offer.

In 1847, he was elected to the Legislative Assembly of the Province of Canada, representing Kingston. Climbing the ranks so quickly in politics requires a sharp intellect, a tactical mind, and profound oratory skills. Macdonald had the first two in plenty, but surprisingly, he hated giving speeches. Probably that's why the people voted for him, seeing his honest self while campaigning.

In 1849, his child, John Jr., passed away. A year later, Isabella gave birth to another boy (Hugh), but Macdonald couldn't get over the loss of his first child. He started drinking heavily and immersed himself in his work.

Throughout the 1850s, he solidified his reputation as a skilled and dependable politician. He served in various ministerial positions, including Receiver General and Attorney General for Canada West (now Ontario), gaining valuable experience in governance and administration.

Macdonald always saw the different provinces of Canada as one entity, and he got the chance to bring his vision into reality with the coalition of 1854. He was responsible for putting together the "Liberal-Conservatives," a party that carried the values of both sides of the spectrum. It was one of his first steps toward the Confederation of Canada. In Canada East (present-day Ontario), he had an ally in George-Étienne Cartier (a French-Canadian politician), who would remain his political partner for nearly 20 years.

In 1857, he was again chosen to lead the Conservatives, but he remained the only candidate from his party in Canada West. Nevertheless, he was a formidable power in the political landscape. Later that year, he suffered a personal loss when Isabella died at the age of 48.

She never recovered from her illness, so her death wasn't unexpected. Nevertheless, it may have intensified John's drinking habit.

His political career didn't suffer, however. During an election debate, his habit became the center of attention. The opposing candidate said, *"Is this the man you want running your country? A drunk!"* Macdonald replied wittily, *"I get sick ... not because of drink [but because] I am forced to listen to the ranting of my honorable opponent."*

Keeping his son, Hugh, under the care of his paternal aunt, he continued to create waves as a Conservative leader. His brilliance can be especially seen while choosing the capital of Canada (West, East, Upper, and Lower).

His opponents and the Assembly wanted Quebec City as the seat of the government, but Macdonald suggested letting the Queen choose. In the interim, he let Quebec City be a temporary capital and requested the Queen delay her decision by 10 months. Thus, he was able to please both the Queen and the men in power in Canada. Eventually, Ottawa was chosen as the permanent capital.

His alliance with George Brown, the leader of the Reform movement (the Liberals), laid the groundwork for the imminent Confederation, as Macdonald sought to bridge the divide between English and French-speaking Canadians and forge a path toward unity. His leadership was especially tested during the early 1860s.

He faced opposition from rival political factions and within his own party, but he proved adept at building consensus and overcoming obstacles. His leadership during this period was characterized by pragmatism, compromise, and a steadfast commitment to uniting the British North American colonies.

By 1864, Sir John A. Macdonald had emerged as one of the most influential political figures in Canada. His vision of Confederation, rooted in the principles of unity, stability, and economic prosperity, resonated with a growing number of Canadians. This period set the stage for his pivotal role in the events that would lead to the creation of Canada as one nation.

Confederation of Canada and the Birth of a Nation

Macdonald's vision of a united Canada began to take shape in 1864. In September, a conference was held in Charlottetown, Prince Edward Island, to discuss a union of the Maritime colonies (Brunswick and Nova Scotia). Representatives from the Province of Canada (Ontario and Quebec) were also invited. Macdonald, as the Premier of the Province of Canada, attended this conference along with other leading politicians. It was here that the idea of a broader union of all British North American colonies took root.

Following the success of the Charlottetown Conference, a second conference was held in Quebec City in October 1864. Delegates from the provinces of Canada, Nova Scotia, New Brunswick, and Prince Edward Island were present. This time, along with the Maritime colonies, a union of the Canadian colonies was discussed. Macdonald played a key role in drafting the 72 Resolutions, which outlined the terms of Confederation. These resolutions formed the basis for the eventual British North America Act of 1867.

Around two years later, Macdonald traveled to London in the company of other colonial leaders to finalize the details of the Confederation with British authorities. The British North America Act received Royal Assent (approved by the Queen) on March 29, 1867. It was a proud moment for John, the other leaders, and the Canadian people when the country united – the Dominion of Canada was born on July 1, 1867. Even today, July 1 is enthusiastically celebrated as Canada Day throughout the country.

Agnes Bernard.
https://commons.wikimedia.org/wiki/File:SABernard.jpg

Another triumph for Macdonald came in the form of Agnes Bernard, who accepted his marriage proposal to become Agnes Macdonald. She was his secretary's sister, and they had been courting for a while. At that moment, it seemed like John was at the top of the world. However, he would scale newer heights and fall to deeper lows in the future.

His Role as the Legendary First Prime Minister

The federal elections were held soon after the Dominion of Canada emerged. Sir John A. Macdonald was the clear and obvious winner, given his vast political experience and acumen and his efforts to unite the country. However, holding on to his position as the first Prime Minister of Canada wasn't easy.

Nova Scotia wanted to withdraw from the union. His efforts to include Newfoundland (a large island to the east) into the fold proved futile. To make matters worse, he got infected with a severe illness.

Mary, his first child with Agnes, arrived as a ray of hope for the Macdonald family. It quickly turned to distress when they realized she could never walk and her brain would not develop beyond a certain age.

PM John tackled all his problems with a brave face. He renewed the deal with Nova Scotia, providing better terms. He shifted his focus to Prince Edward Island and brought it under the Dominion. In an era when disabled children were sent off to health institutes, he learned to love his daughter and care for her despite her shortcomings, lovingly calling her "Baboo." In essence, he had struck a delicate balance between his personal and professional life.

On the professional front, Macdonald was a strong advocate for Canada's expansion and development. His government embarked on ambitious projects like the construction of the Canadian Pacific Railway (CPR), which connected the eastern provinces with the western territories.

Macdonald recognized the importance of a transcontinental railway in uniting Canada geographically, economically, and politically. Due to his efforts as PM, the CPR was successfully completed in 1885.

It revolutionized transportation and commerce in Canada, facilitating the settlement of the western territories, the development of natural resources, and the expansion of trade with Asia. The CPR remains a symbol of Canadian ingenuity, perseverance, and national unity, and Macdonald's leadership played a central role in its construction and legacy.

Under his leadership, Canada expanded its territory through negotiations, purchases, and treaties with Indigenous peoples and other colonial powers. The acquisition of Rupert's Land, the Northwest Territories, and British Columbia into Confederation significantly enlarged Canada's territory and population.

Apart from expansion, Macdonald was also responsible for maintaining law and order during that transition period. He established the North-West Mounted Police, a paramilitary force that upheld the law in North-Western Canada. His government implemented the National Policy, a series of protectionist measures aimed at promoting Canadian industry and boosting economic growth. Key components of this policy were high tariffs on imported goods, subsidies for domestic manufacturing, and the promotion of immigration to settle the western territories.

While controversial at the time, the National Policy played a major role in shaping Canada's economy and society. However, it wasn't the only controversy that haunted this legendary figure. Macdonald served as Canada's prime minister for 19 years until his death, but it wasn't a smooth consecutive tenure.

The Controversies Surrounding His Policies

- **Treatment of Indigenous Peoples:** One of the most significant controversies surrounding Macdonald is his government's treatment of Indigenous peoples. While he did not implement the residential school system, he continued enforcing it during his tenure. This system aimed to assimilate Indigenous children into Euro-Canadian society, which had devastating consequences for Indigenous communities. Apart from losing their culture and identity, they also lost their land and suffered mistreatment in those schools.

- **Chinese Immigration and the Chinese Head Tax:** Macdonald imposed a series of discriminatory measures in an attempt to restrict Chinese immigration to Canada. He enforced a Chinese Head Tax in 1885, which required Chinese immigrants to pay a substantial fee to enter the country. It was motivated by racial prejudice and xenophobia and contributed to the marginalization and exploitation of Chinese immigrants in the Dominion.

- **Pacific Scandal:** In 1872, Macdonald's government became embroiled in the Pacific Scandal. It was revealed that certain members of his party had accepted bribes from businessmen associated with the construction of the Canadian Pacific Railway in exchange for lucrative contracts and political favors. That was when Macdonald stepped down as Prime Minister, but he was re-elected in 1878.

Despite all his controversial decisions, Macdonald successfully held his position until his death. To this day, he has the second-longest tenure as the Prime Minister of Canada (Lyon Mackenzie King held it for the longest period of 21 years), but if he had not died in 1891, he may well have surpassed King's tenure.

Before judging Macdonald for his controversial decisions, it's important to understand the general mentality of the era. Europeans were brought up in a racially discriminated environment. Many held their race on a pedestal, and many others learned to despise other races from childhood. Through that lens, Macdonald's achievements definitely outweigh his controversial policies.

As Sir John A. Macdonald once said, "Anybody may support me when I am right. What I want is someone that will support me when I am wrong. There may be obstructions, local differences may intervene, but it matters not."

Chapter 2: The Arctic Explorations of John Franklin and the Inuit Guides

The Arctic is a polar region in the far north of the Earth where the winter temperature can drop to more than -70°F, and summers can be as cold as the average temperature in Minnesota. It rarely, if ever, rains, but the fierce winds can often cook up an icy storm. The Arctic Ocean, though small and shallow, has towering icebergs that can icebound (freeze in place) ships in a matter of minutes.

The continent is sparsely inhabited, with just over four million residents, less than half the population of New York City. Today, humans have many advanced fabrics and synthetic materials to keep them warm in the Arctic's harsh conditions, but the situation was entirely different two centuries ago when Canada was still separated into provinces, and the region beyond the Arctic Circle was yet to be explored.

John Franklin.

In such vast, unknown terrain, where icy winds whipped across barren landscapes and frigid waters stretched endlessly, one man dared to explore the land that wasn't yet present on any map so far. It was the early 1800s, and the man was called John Franklin.

He ventured into the uncharted Arctic thrice and would have gone a fourth time if he had returned from his final expedition. The mystery surrounding his disappearance captivates explorers and history buffs to this day. Nevertheless, because of Franklin's efforts, a large area of the Arctic was mapped out in the past.

Biography

Sir John Franklin was born on April 16, 1786, in Spilsby, Lincolnshire, England, to Willingham Franklin and Hannah Weekes. He came from a modest background: his father was a merchant, and his mother was the daughter of a farmer. He had 11 siblings, and his elder brothers struggled to achieve success. Hence, initially, he wanted to improve his family's financial situation.

John's younger sister, Sarah, eventually married and gave birth to Emily Sellwood. Emily would go on to marry Alfred Lord Tennyson, one of the greatest poets of the era.

However, while studying at a small-town school closer to the shore, John realized his dream of sailing on the sea and exploring far-off lands. He was inspired by the expeditions of Captain James Cook (a British explorer famous for his voyages to Australia and New Zealand) and dreamed of exploring uncharted regions.

Despite his father's reluctance in his chosen career (he wanted his son to start a business or get into church service), he was given permission to travel on a merchant ship at the tender age of 12. After that, Sir John Franklin never looked back.

He joined the Royal Navy in 1800 at the age of 14, beginning his naval career as a midshipman. During the Napoleonic Wars, he was engaged in several naval strife, including the Battle of Trafalgar in 1805, where he served aboard HMS Bellerophon. He gradually rose through the ranks, gaining valuable experience in seamanship and navigation.

John was married twice and had a daughter from his first wife. His family was a staunch supporter of his dreams and became his main source of motivation for his future explorations. He became battle-hardened in many sea skirmishes and wars, particularly the Battle of Copenhagen, the Battle of Pulo Aura, and the Battle of Lake Borgne, before realizing his dream.

His First Expedition

Since John Franklin had racked up enough experience in the Napoleonic Wars at sea and was passionate about mapping uncharted lands, he was the obvious choice to lead an expedition in the Arctic. The goal was to chart the northern coast of Canada, starting from the mouth of the Coppermine River in Nunavut and then exploring westward.

It was a part of the efforts to find the Northwest Passage, a mythical (at least, back then) route that connected to Asia from that direction (essentially, from the Atlantic to the Pacific), and which explorers had been trying to find since Christopher Columbus' expedition (circa 1500s). The team included Franklin as the leader, George Back as second-in-command, several officers, scientists, and a crew of voyageurs (French-Canadian fur traders and guides) recruited for their experience in navigating Canadian waterways.

The expedition departed from York Factory, a Hudson's Bay Company (HBC, a fur trading business that still exists today) trading post on Hudson Bay, in June 1819.

The HBC was founded on May 2, 1670, by a group of English merchants, including Prince Rupert of the Rhine, with a Royal Charter from King Charles II of England. The charter granted the company exclusive trading rights over the watershed draining into Hudson Bay.

They primarily dealt in beaver pelts since those little furry creatures were more common in the Arctic. When the demand for pelts declined, they scoured further for mink, muskrat, sable marten, and fox fur.

They traveled inland via the Hayes River, where reportedly Franklin accidentally went overboard but was rescued by a crewman. Upon reaching Cumberland House, they gathered additional supplies. The journey to the Coppermine River itself was tiresome and dangerous, as it involved long walks across rough terrain and sailing down fierce rapids.

The explorers reached the mouth of the Coppermine River in July 1821 after facing many hardships and delays along the way. John had believed he would be back home by 1821, but their actual exploration had just begun. The main problem was their dwindling supplies, but they went forward with the expedition by building a crude boat and mapping the coastline westward.

It is said that Franklin and his team encountered several Indigenous locals during their journey, specifically the Yellowknives (Copper Dene). Their leader, named Akaitcho, turned out to be helpful and highly intelligent. He helped them travel further westward and refilled their supplies, but as fate would have it, the winter of that year was especially harsh.

They spent the winter months of 1821–1822 at Fort Enterprise, a makeshift fort constructed near the mouth of the Coppermine River. During this trying time, they ran out of supplies again. The situation eventually worsened so much that they had to eat their leather boots for sustenance. That was how Franklin earned his infamous nickname, "the man who ate his boots."

Hunting wasn't an option since the river barely had any fish, and there wasn't much game around. They needed meat to survive, which may have caused one man from their crew to resort to cannibalism. However, this could be simply speculation because the team mysteriously lost 11 of their men.

They were finally rescued from their deadly situation in October 1821, by which time only four people survived, including John. The rescuers were at a loss for words when they saw the team's plight, but they were recorded saying, *"the ghastly countenances, dilated eyeballs and sepulchral voices of Captain John Franklin and those with him were hard to see and bear."*

Despite facing numerous hardships, Franklin's Coppermine River expedition was a moderate success. He may not have met his goal of reaching Repulse Bay (Naujaat) toward the north, but he mapped a considerable portion of the coast that would help in many future expeditions.

His Second Expedition

It didn't take long for John Franklin to recover from his near-fatal Coppermine River expedition. A year later (circa 1823), he was hale and hearty and ready to marry the woman he loved, a poet named Eleanor Anne Porden. Within a year, they had a daughter, and all seemed to be going well for the family when tragedy struck.

Eleanor Anne Porden.

Eleanor died of tuberculosis in 1825. It wasn't unexpected since she had been suffering from health problems for a long time. However, to help her husband cope with her impending death, she asked him to indulge in his passion for exploration. So, a few days before the fateful day, John Franklin left for his second expedition, keeping the memory of a healthy Eleanor alive.

This time, he would travel further north to the mouth of the Mackenzie River and start mapping the region westward until he met Frederick William Beechey, a fellow explorer. The latter would sail from the Bering Strait eastward to meet John, possibly halfway along the coast.

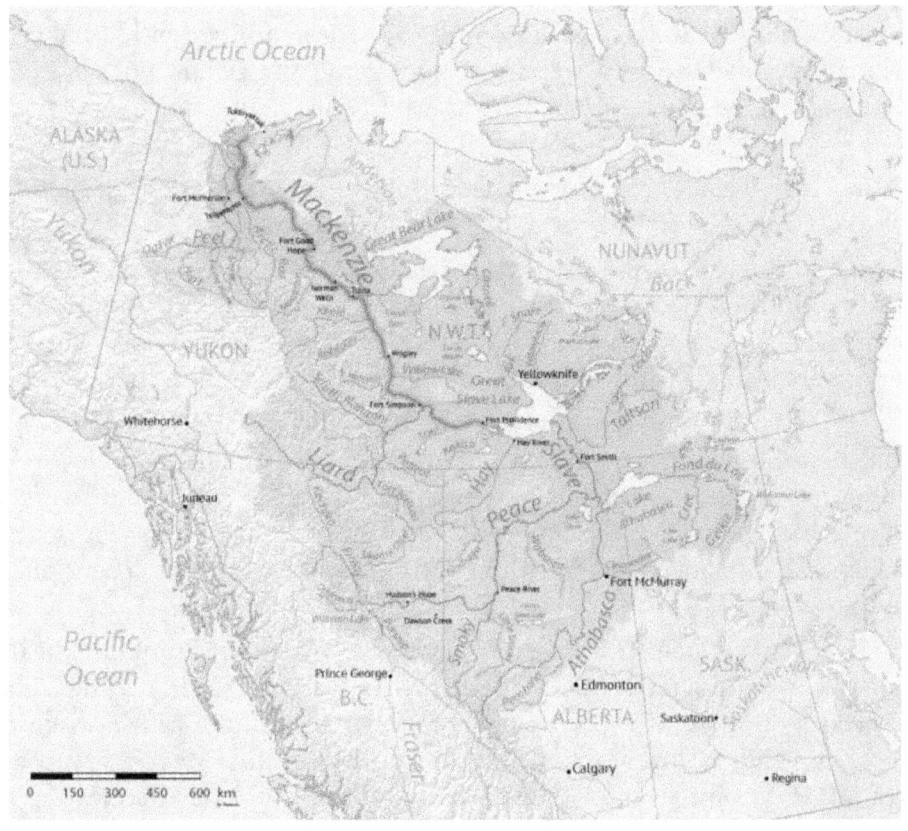

The Mackenzie River on the map.

The planning was meticulous, but the expedition didn't turn out the way either had hoped it would. Learning from the mistakes of his disastrous Coppermine River expedition, Franklin had accounted for almost everything, from the supplies to the gear. However, he hadn't anticipated the ever-changing, treacherous terrain.

His team met with their trusted local allies, the Yellowknives, at Great Slave Lake.

Great Slave Lake is the second-largest lake within Canadian borders, covering an area of approximately 11,030 square miles. It is also the deepest lake in North America, with a maximum depth of 2,014 feet.

Akaitcho wasn't available, so they collaborated with his brother, Keskarrah. In August 1825, John went with them downriver to the mouth of the Mackenzie and came back to winter at a base camp on Great Bear Lake.

The Great Bear Lake was completely frozen in ice, and Franklin's writings say that his men were playing a game he called "hockey," the very first use of the word. This was where the now-popular sport was born.

When he went back downriver the following summer, the ocean was completely frozen on his side.

So, he traveled westward with his team, sailing when he could, but mostly portaging. It was hard work carrying their boat and supplies, but he trudged on. Along the way, he met several Inuit settlements. Most of them were friendly and helpful, but like any community, there were a few bad apples in there.

When the team met the first settlement, many of their supplies were plundered. The second settlement spoke against their fellow Inuit's actions and helped the team refill some of the supplies. They also exchanged gifts and provided directions about a safe route a few miles west.

However, in August, when summer came to a close, Franklin and his men were completely exhausted and could go no further. They had covered a distance of more than 2,000 miles in 80 days with no sign of Beechey's ship on the horizon. If they had known that Beechey was just around 160 miles west at Point Barrow, they would have gone on. In John Franklin's own words, "No difficulties, dangers, or discouraging circumstances should have prevented him from meeting Beechey."

However, hoping to avoid a repeat of the Coppermine River expedition and not knowing how far Beechey was, Franklin made the immensely difficult decision of heading back to the Mackenzie. Another team under a fellow explorer, John Richardson, went east from the Mackenzie to meet William Edward Parry, who sailed west from the Atlantic. Both of them successfully mapped the area with barely any mishaps.

His Final Fateful Expedition

After he returned from his second expedition in 1827, John Franklin courted and married Jane Griffin (a friend of Eleanor, his first wife) in about a year. They had a lot in common because, like John, Jane loved to travel around the world. She had already visited many parts of Europe before her marriage, so she understood John's motivations for taking the third voyage to the Arctic despite nearing 60 years of age.

Due to his age, he wasn't the first choice of the British higher-ups. The honor was given to Sir James Clark Ross, another seasoned explorer who had led an expedition to Antarctica. When he declined the honor, their second choice was Franklin, who accepted. As they say, one man's loss is another man's gain. Given the fate of the expedition, Franklin may have lost more than he gained with the acceptance.

The expedition consisted of two ships, HMS Erebus and HMS Terror, along with a crew of 129 men.

After Franklin's moderately successful first and second expeditions, a little over 300 miles of Arctic coastline were to be explored. To minimize the risk of starvation, health problems, or death, like in the first one, he ensured that his ships and men were equipped with the latest technology for the age.

The ships ran on powerful steam engines and were equipped with steam-based distillation and heating systems to maintain the health of the crew. The food supplies could last them comfortably for three whole years, and they had thousands of books to read for whiling away their time. Franklin and his men were given heavy wool coats, trousers, and undergarments. Fur-lined parkas, boots, mittens, and hats were also provided.

Franklin and his crew departed from England in May 1845. Their objective was to chart the remaining 300 miles of the coastline and find the fabled Northwest Passage connecting the Atlantic to the Pacific. They first traveled north to Scotland for additional supplies, then west to Greenland, and finally toward the Canadian Arctic islands after departing from Disko Island near Greenland.

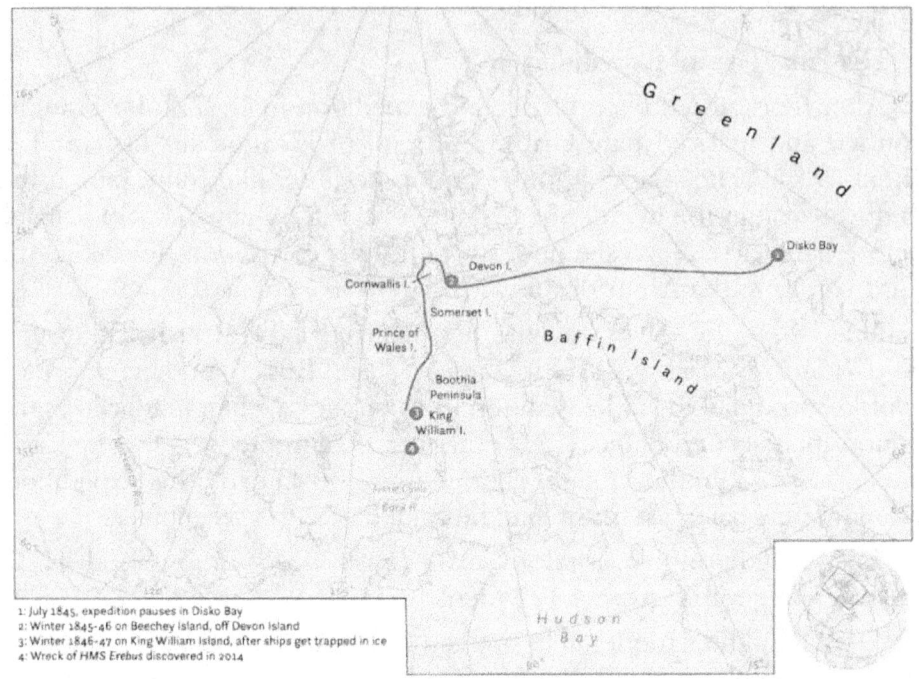

A line tracing of Franklin's journey from Disko Island to the Arctic Islands of Devon.
Hans van der Maarel, CC BY-SA 4.0 <https://creativecommons.org/licenses/by-sa/4.0>, via Wikimedia Commons. https://commons.wikimedia.org/wiki/File:Franklin%27s-Lost-Expedition.png

After that, their ships weren't seen by any European eyes. Two years passed by, and Lady Franklin grew worried. She wanted the Royal Navy to send a search expedition, but since Franklin and the crew had three years of supplies, they waited another year before sending search parties.

Over the next few years, many ships were dispatched to locate the explorers, but they found no sign of the lost ships or their crew. Ultimately, between 1854 and 1859, many indications of the explorers' fate were found. In particular, a message left by members of the expedition was discovered, indicating that Franklin had died in 1847 and that the surviving crew had abandoned the ships in a desperate attempt to reach safety on foot.

After more than 160 years, in September 2014, the remains of HMS Erebus were found near the Adelaide Peninsula. Two years later, HMS Terror was located near King William Island in better condition than Erebus. These rediscoveries happened all because of the Inuit people's help.

The Invaluable Contributions of the Inuit

If it weren't for the Inuit (natives of the North American Arctic), the fate of Franklin's Northwest Passage expedition may have remained a mystery forever. It so happened that after several search parties failed to find anything about Franklin's lost expedition, John Rae, a Scottish explorer, stumbled upon a group of Inuit peoples who had some idea about the crew's fate.

They told Rae that the two ships became icebound near the Boothia Peninsula. The crew tried to walk in search of a safe haven, but many died due to the extreme cold. The remaining few were forced to eat their flesh to keep themselves alive, but they, too, eventually met their deaths.

The wildlife in the Boothia Peninsula is scarce but not entirely non-existent. Polar bears, foxes, reindeer, Arctic hares, and seals can often be found roaming on the snow-covered landscape. However, Franklin's crew may barely have had any strength to hunt for the game.

Rae and the Royal Navy tried to keep cannibalism under wraps, but it was leaked to the press and caused great uproar in society. Later, in 1997, when the remains of some of the crew were found on King William Island (preserved in the snow), the Inuit story of cannibalism was confirmed when many blade marks were detected on their bodies. It shows that humans are indeed capable of anything in extreme situations.

Franklin's body, however, was buried by the crew according to the 1859 message, but the location wasn't marked, and it hasn't yet been found at the time of writing this. Research has shown that the main causes of the crew's death were pneumonia, tuberculosis, and lead poisoning. The latter may have been caused by faulty canned food or a damaged water distillation system.

The Inuit aid didn't end there. They were also responsible for helping to find the exact location of the ships. Inuit oral traditions passed down stories of encounters with the expedition members and knowledge of the ship's whereabouts. These stories were often dismissed by European explorers and search parties at the time but proved to be valuable clues in later searches.

They knew the region's geography, ice conditions, and wildlife inside-out and helped the search parties attempting to navigate the treacherous Arctic waters to locate the missing ships. Over the centuries, they also discovered and preserved various artifacts belonging to Franklin's expedition, such as tools, clothing, and personal items. The location of these items greatly narrowed down the search, leading to the famous rediscovery in 2014 and 2016.

In recent years, Canada has recognized the importance of indigenous knowledge and engagement in Arctic governance and sovereignty. The Inuit play a crucial role in Canada's Arctic policy development, resource management, and environmental protection.

Legacy

The Northwest Passage expedition became one of the most infamous tragedies in the history of Arctic exploration. The loss of Franklin and his crew captured the public's imagination, leading to many bizarre theories and speculations about their fate. It may seem like a futile expedition on the surface, serving only to spawn and feed fantastical rumors, but it had several unintended advantages.

The search parties that tried to find the lost ships may not have achieved their goal, but they were able to map the region thoroughly, achieving Franklin's goal instead. They managed to develop a symbiotic relationship with the Inuit, exchanging gifts and getting valuable help during their explorations.

Franklin's expedition and the subsequent search efforts involved international cooperation between Canada, the United Kingdom, the United States, and others. This collaboration continues today through organizations like the Arctic Council, where Canada participates in discussions on Arctic governance, environmental protection, and sustainable development alongside other Arctic nations.

Furthermore, the Europeans got to know more about Inuit culture, the wildlife thriving in the region, and the weather patterns. The Inuit also taught them useful techniques for surviving in harsh conditions. John Franklin's lost expedition only seems like a failure, but it was, in fact, an indisputable success.

Chapter 3: Viola Desmond and Nellie McClung's Fight for Equality

Women in the 21st century owe so much to those who came before them. Throughout history, many female figures fought for equality and social justice so future generations would have equal rights and freedom to vote. They stood against racism and sexism to silence the voices that treated them as second-class citizens.

Throughout history, many female figures fought for equality and social justice.
https://commons.wikimedia.org/wiki/File:Womanpower_logo.svg

Modern-day Canada's diverse, inclusive, and tolerant culture is a far cry from its bleak history. The country would have looked much different today if it weren't for the people who spoke up against discrimination.

Viola Desmond and Nellie McClung were two women who refused to live in an unjust world. They chose to make a difference, and what they achieved changed Canada forever.

This chapter tells the inspiring stories of their fight for civil rights and women's suffrage in Canada.

Viola Desmond

Viola Desmond was an African-Canadian businesswoman. Her story is similar to that of African-American activist Rosa Parks. Both women defied authority and challenged racism by refusing to move from their seats in the "White-only" sections, which led to their arrest. Their heroic actions contributed to the civil rights movements in both countries.

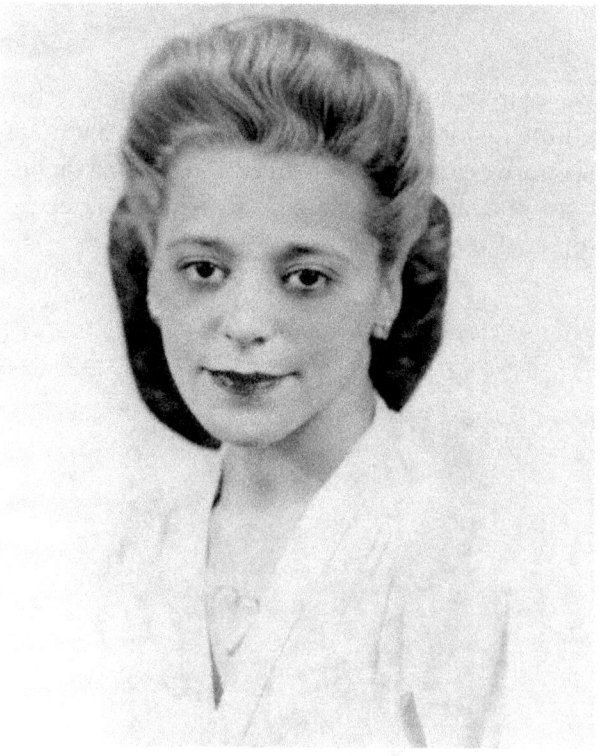

Viola Desmond.
https://commons.wikimedia.org/wiki/File:Viola_Desmond.jpg

Viola Desmond Biography

Viola Irene Davis, AKA Viola Desmond, was born on July 6, 1914, in Halifax, Nova Scotia. Her mother, a White woman, Gwendolyn Irene Johnson, was a housewife, and her father, a Black man, James Davis, was a businessman. They had eleven children together.

Biracial couples were uncommon at the time and were subjected to racial slurs and attacks. However, her parents were highly respected members of the Black community who embraced them and their children.

Viola attended a racially mixed school, and her teachers described her as an exceptional student. She wanted to become a teacher, but Black people weren't allowed to take teacher educational programs. She had to take a provincial test to earn her certificate. She worked at a segregated Black school in Halifax's Black community.

Many of her students were Black Americans who escaped from the oppression and discrimination in the U.S. to the promise of a better future in Canada. However, they soon realized the ugly reality that racism in Canada was no different from America.

Black people weren't allowed to own land and homes or serve on a jury. They were also denied entry to churches and other places of worship, and some hospitals and doctors refused to treat them. Restaurants, taverns, and hotels across the country denied them service.

Black Canadians felt excluded from their society, so they built their own churches, schools, and businesses. Viola felt angry and oppressed as she witnessed the discrimination against her people. A fire burned inside of her that would soon erupt and change many Black Canadians' lives.

Ever since Viola was a little girl, she dreamed of opening a beauty salon. She wanted to have her own business like her father. Beauty schools in Halifax didn't accept students of African descent, but she didn't let that stop her from achieving her goals.

Viola traveled to Montreal to attend the Field Beauty Culture School, which accepted Black students, and she completed her training in New York. She returned to Halifax and, at the age of 32, used the money she earned from her teaching job to open her beauty salon, Vi's Studio of Beauty Culture. Viola married Jack Desmond, and they had two children.

Vi's Studio served Black women in her community who were excited to finally find a salon that didn't discriminate against them. Viola became very successful and created her own makeup line.

Viola didn't want other young girls to face the same challenges she did, so she started the Desmond School of Beauty Culture, the only beauty school in Halifax for Black women. Many girls earned their degrees from Viola's school. She also supported them until they finished their education and helped them find jobs.

She opened multiple branches of her salon across Nova Scotia and was highly respected in the Black community. Viola had a great life with her loving family and thriving business. However, this was all about to change.

The Roseland Theatre Incident

On November 8, 1946, Viola was traveling alone for a business meeting when her car broke down in New Glasgow, Nova Scotia. The repair shop told her it would take hours to fix it, so she decided to pass the time and see a movie at the Roseland Theater.

She asked for a main-floor ticket, but the ticket seller ignored her request and gave her a balcony one instead. Viola didn't know that the theater was segregated; Black people were prohibited from sitting in the lower section. They were only allowed to sit in the balcony seats.

Unknowingly, she went to sit in the main area, but the usher told her that she had the wrong seat and should move to the balcony. She thought there was a mistake and went to exchange the ticket.

The Roseland Theatre.

However, the ticket seller told her, *"I'm sorry, but I'm not permitted to sell downstairs tickets to you people."* His words left her shocked and appalled. She realized she was being discriminated against for her skin color and decided to take a stand.

She sat in the main area, defying the theater's rules. The usher threatened to call the manager, but Viola told him, *"Get the manager. I'm not doing anything wrong."* Henry MacNeil, the theater's manager, confronted Viola and told her, *"The theater had the right to refuse admission to any objectionable person."* However, Viola still refused to leave her seat.

Henry called the police, and she was dragged out of the theater. She described the incident, saying, *"The policeman grasped my shoulders, and the manager grabbed my legs, injuring my knee and hip. They carried me bodily from the theater, out into the street."* She spent the night in a cell.

Viola was sad and scared. What began as a pleasant evening where she would watch a nice movie ended with her being humiliated and in jail.

The Trial

Viola was taken to court the next morning. She didn't have a lawyer, and the court did not appoint one. She was charged with defrauding the government for refusing to pay a one-cent amusement tax, the difference between the lower-seat ticket and the balcony ticket. She told the judge, "I offered to pay the difference; they would not accept it." However, the judge ignored her testimony and fined her $26, six of which were given to the theater's manager.

During the proceedings, the judge didn't mention the race issue.

The Impact of the Roseland Theatre Incident

Jack, Viola's husband, grew up in New Glasgow, so he was accustomed to racial segregation. He told her not to fight the system and to "Take it to the Lord with a prayer." This was the opinion of a few people in Nova Scotia. However, others were angry at the treatment Viola faced.

The Nova Scotia Association for the Advancement of Coloured People (NSAACP) raised money to help Viola appeal her case. Black journalist Carrie Best, the founder of The Clarion newspaper, published her story on the paper's front page.

Viola's story spread across Canada and the U.S. An article titled *"Assaulted and Hurt by Canada"* was published in the American newspaper *The Baltimore Afro-American* on February 1, 1947.

Viola's doctor advised her to sue the theater and their manager on account of her injuries. She hired a White lawyer, Frederick Bissett. Since the Canadian court had never ruled against racial discrimination before, Frederick sued the theater and its manager and demanded compensation for her assault and false imprisonment.

However, the case didn't go to trial. He also tried to have her criminal conviction expunged, but the court declined. Frederick didn't bill Viola for his work, so the NSAACP used the money they raised to fight against racism and segregation.

Segregation was outlawed in Nova Scotia in 1954, thanks to people like Viola Desmond, whose determination and fight for equality created the Canada you know today. However, Viola's defiance came at a price. She and Jack divorced, and she left her business in New York, where she died alone at the age of 50.

She became a prominent Canadian public figure, with her picture featured on the Canadian ten-dollar bill and a postage stamp.

Viola never intended to be an activist, but she believed that one small step could make a big difference. *"Do your little bit of good where you are. It's those little bits of good put together that overwhelm the world."*

Carrie Best

Carrie Best was a human rights activist and journalist. She was born on March 4, 1903, in New Glasgow, Nova Scotia. Best founded The Clarion, the first Canadian newspaper owned by a Black person. She spent her life advocating for equality and social justice for Black people. She was especially interested in Viola's story because she experienced a similar incident in the same theater.

In 1941, she heard that a group of high school Black girls were dragged from the theater for sitting in the "White people" section. She went to the theater with her son and requested a main-floor ticket but was given a balcony one. She went to sit in the main area, defying the theater's rules.

The theater's assistant manager called the police, and she and her son were forcibly removed from the theater. She was convicted and fined for disturbing the peace.

A. E. Waddell, Chairman

A. T. Best, The Clarion

Clarion Celebrates its First Birthday

On July 28th, the Clarion celebrated its first birthday. A good deal of progress has been made since the first single sheet made a week and shaky appearance over a year ago. Today that single sheet has grown to eight pages, and the venture of one person has become a full fledged company.

This venture has not been without its disappointments and failures, yet we are certain that a great need in the cultural and educational life of colored Maritimers is being served.

Originally the Clarion was designed as a Church bulletin, with a little local news added for variety, but it soon became apparent from the demand from outside New Glasgow that this was not enough. Consequently we branched out bit by bit.

Today, even with our eight pages we are forced to omit news that we would

like to print, in order to give a fair coverage to each community.

We mentioned in a foregoing paragraph that the Clarion was now a company. Perhaps our readers would like to know some more about the people who formed that company and gave it their support.

The Chairman of the Board of Directors is Dr. A. E. Waddell, well known Halifax physician. Dr. Waddell has been one of the most consistent boosters of the Clarion, and suggested the formation of the company at a time when it was feared that the Clarion was doomed to fail. His help has been of tremendous value to the editors.

The Treasurer of the company is Mr. L. D. Mills of New Glasgow. Mr. Mills has been a steady backer of the Clarion, and but for his encouragement it would have been indeed hard to go on.

Continued on page 8

Carrie Best is on the top left.

https://commons.wikimedia.org/wiki/File:The_Clarion,_volume_2,_number_11,_page_3.jpg

Wanda Robson

After Viola's death, her younger sister, Wanda, kept her legacy alive. Born on December 16, 1926, in Halifax, Wanda made history by clearing her sister's name and getting her pardoned for her defraud case. This was the first time a Canadian person received a posthumous pardon. Wanda also wrote books, did interviews, and spoke to college students to explain her sister's role in the Canadian civil rights movement.

Timeline of Legal Changes in Canada's Civil Rights

- In 1934, Manitoba passed a Libel Act to prevent racial attacks.
- In 1944, Ontario passed the Racial Discrimination Act prohibiting the display of racial symbols or signs.
- In 1945, The B.C. Social Assistance Act prohibited racial discrimination.
- In 1947, Tommy Douglas passed the Saskatchewan Bill of Rights prohibiting discrimination.
- In 1948, the Federal Elections Act allowed people of all races to vote.
- In 1964, Ontario abolished the laws for segregated schools.
- In 1971, it became a crime to initiate hatred or violent attacks against Black people.

Nellie McClung

Nellie was a women's rights activist and suffragette who dedicated her life to granting women equal rights.

Nellie McClung Biography

Helen Letitia Mooney, AKA Nellie McClung, was born on October 20, 1873, in Chatsworth, Ontario, to John Mooney and Letitia McCurdy. At the age of seven, she and her family moved to Souris Valley, Manitoba, where she grew up on a homestead. She started going to school at the age of ten. However, she was a clever girl and received a teaching certificate at the age of 16. She started her fight against inequality at a young age when she joined different social reform groups.

Nellie McClung.

She worked as a teacher at a school near Manitoba for seven years until 1896, when she met and married pharmacist Robert Wesley McClung. The couple lived a happy life together and had five children.

Nellie's mother-in-law was president of the Woman's Christian Temperance Union, which advocated reducing alcohol consumption. She often took her daughter-in-law to meetings, and soon, she became an active and prominent member. Her work with the union ignited her interest in the women's suffrage movement.

She published her first novel, *"Sowing Seeds in Danny,"* in 1908. It is a humorous story about a small western town. It quickly became a best-seller, making Nellie one of Canada's most famous authors. She went on to write articles and short stories in Canadian and American publications.

Fighting for Women's Suffrage

In 1911, Nellie, her husband, and their children moved to Winnipeg, where she became a public speaker and got involved in politics. She joined the Winnipeg women's rights and reform movement to fight for women's suffrage from 1911 to 1914. She described her time in Winnipeg, saying, *"The big city gathered us in ... I enjoyed my association with the Canadian Women's Press Club. There, great problems were discussed, and the seed germ of the suffrage association was planted. We felt we should organize and create public sentiment in favor of women's suffrage."*

She became popular among many women – thanks to her exceptional public speaking skills and sense of humor. Her words were powerful and resonated with many women at the time: *"I am a believer in women, in their ability to do things and in their influence and power. Women set the standards for the world, and it is for us, women in Canada, to set the standards high."*

In 1914, she supported the Liberal Party against the Conservative government, which denied women the right to vote. She also participated in organizing the Winnipeg Political Equality League to help working women.

Nellie used her wit, sense of humor, and charm to mock Canadian Prime Minister Sir Rodmond Roblin in a parody to highlight the ridiculousness of denying women the right to vote. Her efforts worked, and the Liberal Party won against Rodmond Roblin and his government.

In 1915, she moved with her family to Alberta, where she continued fighting for various reforms, such as a wife's right to a dower after her husband's death, factory safety legislation, and women's suffrage.

She gained recognition in Britain and the U.S. and became a member of the Liberal Legislative Assembly in Alberta from 1921 to 1926.

The Persons Case

Nellie joined a group called *"The Famous Five,"* which included Irene Parlby, Louise Crummy McKinney, Henrietta Muir Edwards, and Emily Murphy. They were activists working on the Persons Case to get women recognized as qualified persons under the law, granting them seats in public offices.

The British North America Act (BNA Act) only recognized persons as males, and according to the Act, only such persons were allowed official positions.

The Supreme Court denied their request in 1928. However, the women didn't give up and continued petitioning and appealing – but they were met with rejection. In 1928, the British Privy Council reversed the Supreme Court decision and ruled in favor of the Famous Five.

The council declared, *"The exclusion of women from all public offices is a relic of days more barbarous than ours. And to those who would ask why the word 'persons' should include females, the obvious answer is, why should it not?"*

This was a great victory for Nellie and all women. Soon after, the Canadian Senate appointed Cairine Wilson, the first female senator.

Later Career

In 1933, Nellie moved with her family to Vancouver Island, where she focused on her writing. She published her autobiography, *"Clearing in the West: My Own Story"* in 1935. She continued writing short stories and articles in magazines and newspapers. She became the League of Nations delegate in 1938 and continued her public speaking career advocating for women's rights.

Nellie died on September 1, 1951, at the age of 77.

Emily Murphy

Emily was born on March 14, 1868, in Innisfil, Canada. She was an author, an activist, and a prominent member of the suffrage movement. In 1916, she became the first Canadian female magistrate. However, on her first day on the job, a lawyer told her that she wasn't recognized as a person under British law. She fought against this injustice by starting the "Persons Case."

Henrietta Muir Edwards

Henrietta was born on December 18, 1849, in Montreal. She was an artist, reformer, and advocate for women's rights. She fought for women's rights to education and work. She joined different organizations and movements that helped women make their own choices and lead better lives. She also contributed to passing the 1917 Alberta Dower Act.

Louise McKinney

Louise was born on September 22, 1868, in Elizabethtown-Kitley, Canada. She was a lay preacher and women's rights activist. She was the first female legislator in Canada and Britain. She was a suffragist and played a role with Henrietta in passing the 1917 Alberta Dower Act. She was a member of the Woman's Christian Temperance Union, which prohibited alcohol and fought for women's right to vote. She worked with the Dominion WCTU to advocate for women's suffrage. In 1916, women in Alberta were granted the right to vote, thanks to her contributions.

Irene Parlby

Irene was born on January 9, 1868, in London, UK. She was a women's rights activist and a member of the Alberta Legislative Assembly (ALA). She was the first Canadian woman to hold a cabinet position. She spent her career advocating for women's rights and helping them secure the same opportunities as men. She passed legislation to enhance the Dower Act, granting mothers allowance and minimum wage for women.

Irene Parlby.

Timeline of Legal Changes in Canadian Women's Voting Rights

- In 1916, acts amending the Manitoba Election Act, the Saskatchewan Statute Law, and an act for Equal Suffrage in Alberta were passed.

- In 1917, acts amending the British Columbia Elections Act, the Ontario Election Act, The War-time Elections Act, and the Military Voters Act were passed.

- In 1918, acts amending the Nova Scotia Franchise Act and the Electoral Franchise upon Women Act were passed.

- In 1919, the New Brunswick Election Act was amended, and the Yukon Election Ordinance was passed.

- In 1922, the Prince Edward Island Election Act was passed.

- In 1925, an act amending the Newfoundland and Labrador Act was passed.

- In 1940, an Act was passed allowing women the right to vote in Quebec.

- In 1951, the Elections Ordinance Act was passed.

- In 1960, the Indian Act and the Canadian Election Act were amended.

Without the perseverance and courage of women like Viola and Nellie, women today would still be fighting for their basic rights. They faced racism and societal and political challenges so future generations would have better lives. These selfless women didn't want fame or recognition; they only wanted to be treated as equals.

Chapter 4: Grey Owl's Journey from England to the Heart of Canadian Conservation

Some claim him to be the greatest environmentalist of the early 20th century. Others call him an impostor. The identity of Grey Owl was shrouded in mystery until his death, and many aspects of his life are still unknown today. However, his contributions to environmentalism and his incredible character have an undeniable impact on early Canadian conservation efforts. As yet another addition to the list of figures who shaped Canadian history, this chapter explores the life and actions of Grey Owl, tracing his path from his home country to his self-fabricated Indigenous identity and beyond.

Grey Owl.
https://commons.wikimedia.org/wiki/File:Grey_Owl.jpg

Who Was Grey Owl?

Born as Archibald Belaney in Hastings, England, in 1888, Grey Owl hadn't had the easiest start in life. When he was a toddler, his parents left England, searching for a better life in the United States, leaving Archibald in the care of his aunts and grandmother. While his relatives provided him with shelter, food, and education, he still felt the void left by his parents, which, according to some, might explain why he found it easy to fabricate his parent's (and own) identity later in life.

After finishing grammar school, Archibald found a job at a local timber factory, where he worked until his move to Canada in 1906. Not yet 18, young Archie was very adventurous and ambitious, and to him, becoming a fur trapper in Northern Ontario seemed like the perfect way to earn a living. After his move, he lived with the Ojibwe people near Lake Temagami, who taught him everything he needed to know about fishing and trapping. In this exciting new world, Archibald became fascinated with the Indigenous way of living. Everything from the culture to how people connected to their environment interested him.

Still looking for more adventures, Archibald joined the Canadian Overseas Expeditionary Force soon after World War I broke out. Around this time, he had already begun refabricating his identity – as his enlistment documents list Montreal as his birthplace. He also claimed to be of First Nation heritage.

While prone to modifying behavior, Archibald's solitary nature and interest in field craft soon evoked his superior's interest in making him a sniper. They encouraged him to improve his rifle skills and use his mobility to his advantage. He listened and trained himself to become a skilled marksman, capable of taking down any number of enemies one by one.

Besides being an extraordinary sniper, his comrades praised him for his bravery, especially during the battle that eventually left him injured and out of service. In a stroke of coincidence, he was taken to a Hastings military hospital to recover – but he didn't stay there or in England, for that matter. In 1917, he was already back in Canada, ready to see more of the Indigenous way of life and continue adopting his new persona.

Grey Owl Is Born

After his return to Canada, Archibald Belaney already claimed to have been born in Hermosillo, Mexico, to a Scottish scout and a Jicarilla Apache woman named Katherine Cochise. His father, George Belaney, served in the Southwestern Indian wars, where he met Buffalo Bill Cody, the wise Indigenous fighter who became his friend. According to Archibald's testimony, Buffalo Bill invited his parents to see the Wild West Show in England. After conceiving him in England, his parents returned to Mexico just before his birth. Soon after he was born, Archibald's family moved to North America. He claimed to have left his family home at the age of 15 when he moved to try his luck at trapping and wood-crafting in Ontario. He also affirmed that the Ojibway people adopted him and gave him a new name, Wa-Sha-Quon-Asin, which translates as *He-Who-Flies-by-Night* or *Grey Owl*. By some accounts, his Indigenous name, given traditionally by one's character, was bestowed because his drive for solitary life further increased after the war. As it happened to many other soldiers, his injuries and experience on the battlefield left their mark on him. However, whether this was true or not, his new name would prove to be an excellent one – especially in light of what he would achieve later in life.

The more time he spent in the woods and rivers of the north, the more Grey Owl had adopted his new persona. He would spend time only with Indigenous people and, sometimes, even refuse to speak English at all. He was described as a temperamental man who, wanting to avoid trouble with the law of whites, chose to isolate himself. At the same time, his Indigenous friends found him to be a good person with a great sense of humor.

Besides being brought down by heavy bouts of melancholy, Grey Owl was further devastated by the changes in the north woods of Canada. By this time, industrialization was in full swing, which meant an increase in wood usage. The forests he came to know as the back of his hands after his first arrival were becoming unrecognizable. In some places, it was overlooked, while in others, the animals disappeared. It made making a living as a fur trapper very troublesome, although this was becoming the least of Grey Owls' concerns. He was also making enemies among the forest inspectors and was facing potential imprisonment for assaulting a station agent.

Amid all this chaos and misfortune, in 1925, Grey Owl met Anahareo, a young Mohawk Iroquois woman who cultivated a deep hatred against the practice of trapping. Also known as Gertrude Bernard, Anahareo was to become the love of Grey Owl's life and the person he was influenced by the most throughout his later years. She showed him the true effect of trapping on the Canadian fauna and encouraged him to learn more about conservation.

It all began when Grey Owl captured and killed a beaver, only to discover that the animal had two young to feed. Anahareo asked him to take in the orphaned beavers and care for them. After doing so, he grew much more compassionate toward the animals, making him leave trapping behind once and for all. It also kicked off his career as a protector and conservationist, as he began his activism in defense of beavers and other wildlife. His newfound sensibility toward animals was also evident in his writing:

"They seemed to be almost like little folk from some other planet, whose language we could not yet quite understand," he wrote. "To kill such creatures seemed monstrous. I would do no more of it. Instead of persecuting them further, I would study them, see just what there really was to them. I perhaps could start

a colony of my own; these animals could not be permitted to pass completely from the face of this wilderness."

First Conservation Efforts and Public Engagement

During the winter that marked the transition between 1928 and 1929, Grey Owl established his first beaver colony and started advocating for it. The initial colony was created with the two kittens Grey Owl and Anahareo raised but was soon expanded with the help of other Indigenous friends. Meanwhile, opting to combine the useful with the pleasant, he reached out to resorts to earn money as a lecturer about conservation. Due to his preference for a solitary lifestyle, public speaking didn't come easy to him, but eventually (and probably fueled by his passion), he found his stride, and the public was enchanted by him. They also paid him well. For one single engagement, he would earn more than he and Anahareo made during an entire trapping season.

With his reputation as a passionate conservationist growing, Grey Owl also took to writing. He crafted articles and books, and in 1930, even contributed to the making of a short film created by the National Parks of Canada about his work in Beaver conservation. He also obtained the support of the Canadian Parks Branch and the Canadian Forestry Association.

Interestingly enough, his first book, *The Men of the Last Frontier*, was first published in England rather than in Canada. However, later on, it became successful in Canada and the United States. After writing his second book, *Pilgrims of the Wild*, the Canadian government made more short films about his work with beavers. This book retells the story of his transformation from a trapper struggling to make a living in an environment devastated by overlogging, fires, and overhunting to an avid animal advocate. It describes his daily life with his two rescue beaver kittens, often describing their humorous adventures growing up.

He was also invited on a lecture tour across Britain. An embodiment of contradiction, he would appear wearing his hair in the traditional two-braid style, along with a sombrero, moccasins, and a conservative suit. Combined with his energetic lecturing manner, he created quite a sensation – just as he did in Canada beforehand. His presumed First Nations identity further added to his allure and success in his efforts to bring the issue of wildlife conservation closer to the broader public.

Public success notwithstanding, even his writing seemed contradictory at times. For example, in some reflections, he would convey his distaste for killing innocent creatures. In others, he confessed to intruding into the territory of animals he professed to protect – or seemed at a loss when he observed the behavior of the beavers he rescued. However, this could be explained with one simple fact. Unlike popular literature, which focused on engagingly portraying the Indigenous lifestyle, his notes shoved the reality of what Indigenous people in the north woods of Canada faced. He had inside knowledge of the effects of industrialization on forestry and wanted everyone to hear and read about it.

Still, he was also known to exaggerate in his nature stories. For instance, in his effort to bring forest creatures closer to the audiences (and make them care for their conservation more), he would make up outrageous tales of encountering up to 58 wolves while hiking in a national park. According to his own accords, despite shooting at them, they would only come threateningly close – only to let him escape without any injury in the end.

Earning Government Support

In the spring of 1931, Grey Owl relocated to Riding Mountain National Park. He was off to a new adventure, taking only a young male beaver with him, while Anahareo was left behind to focus on prospecting. Seeing genuine efforts (and putting aside his somewhat contradictory public persona), the Canadian government offered a job to Grey Owl. He was to work in the park while growing a new beaver colony.

Riding Mountain National Park.
Jamie B. from USA, CC BY 2.0 <https://creativecommons.org/licenses/by/2.0>, via Wikimedia Commons. https://commons.wikimedia.org/wiki/File:Riding_mountain_national_park_3_-_reflection.jpg

Grey Owl gladly accepted, but with one condition – he wanted to choose where to set up camp for himself and his colony. While the park's superintendent suggested that they could live near the largest lake (thinking it would provide plenty of nourishment for the animals), Grey Owl rejected this idea because the spot was too close to the park's boundaries. After spending years observing beavers, he knew that the young specimens often migrated during the spring, and they could easily wander away from the safe confines of the national park. Opting for a small lake instead, he provided more isolation for the beavers.

He made his first conservation effort in the Riding Mountain National Park before fully moving in. Courtesy of the government, a cabin was erected for Grey Owl at his preferred spot, providing an excellent view of the park and more than enough inspiration for his future writings. After a season, he gave a vivid description of the park (bringing it closer in the eyes of other conservation supporters):

"With its poplar forest and rolling downs carpeted with myriad flowers, that stands like an immense island of green above the hot, dry sameness of the wheat-stricken Manitoba prairie that surrounds it."

In this unique description, his Ojibway education shone through, regardless of where his life path may have begun before merging into his fabricated persona.

Unfortunately, after this same season, Grey Owl also realized that the Riding Mountain National Park was too hostile for beavers. He argued it was too isolated and hot and provided little room for young beavers to migrate safely (the beavers he took with him just had their young). Wanting to take his overbearing plan elsewhere, he asked to be transferred. His request was granted, and he and his beaver family were relocated to Ajawaan Lake in Prince Albert National Park, Saskatchewan. He lived there until his death on April 13, 1938.

The Truth Emerges

Soon after Grey Owl's death, the truth about his English origins was revealed. It came to light that he was not Indigenous at all and had never been to Hermosillo – along with many other lies he told over the years. His mother was not Apache but English, and her name was Katherine Cox. His father, George Belaney, was known for scheming ways, having married several times in secret, abandoning several children, and defrauding employers and business associates in both England and the United States. His great uncle, James Belaney, was an avid falcon hunter, so it's safe to say that both fantasy and hunting were inherited passions for Grey Owl, or Archibald Belaney, as was his true name.

Archibald grew up reading stories about the Indigenous people of North America and was an animal lover from an early age. He spent a lot of time imitating animal sounds, eventually learning to hoot like an owl. It was also revealed that he had excellent acting skills, which explains why he was able to charm the public with his fake persona. Spending his free time in St. Helen's Woods, he always sported a tan, which grew even darker during his life in the Canadian north. With all these characteristics, he had everything to sell his apparent First Nation identity.

Grey Owl's Environmental Legacy

Fortunately for the future of Canadian conservation, Grey Owl used his powers of persuasion to create a lasting environmental legacy. After his move from the Riding Mountain National Park, the Canadian authorities decided to implement his original plan and started reintroducing beavers to the park. Their efforts were met with success. Beaver colonies, decimated by trappers in the 18th century, soon began to flourish and thrive in the park. The growth of the beaver population also ensured other animals, like the wolf who fed on them, would thrive as well.

However, just as Grey Owl warned, migrating youngsters moved to wheat farmland beyond the park's limits. They dammed streams on private lands, which caused farmers to shoot and kill them. The authorities received yet another lesson in conservation from Grey Owl. They had to ensure the beaver population not only grew but could do so safely. Otherwise, the dam-happy animals would create a high water reservoir in the middle of a plain. Soon, the park wardens were instructed to blow larger beaver dams to prevent water accumulation on the farmlands of the plains.

Grey Owl might have been full of falsity or imperfections, but he knew how to capture the public's imagination. He knew how to bring very real environmental issues to the front much more efficiently than any politician or environmental burkart of his time could. Moreover, his efforts also shed light on a problem that still persists in modern times. More people who fight for conservation courses are needed. Grey Owl's writings and carefully curated public speeches were all aimed to push people into taking action. He highlighted the importance of preserving nature, considering it a seed of life.

His persona might have been the embodiment of fiction, but his fiction allowed even urban audiences to see what was going on behind the great machine of the Industrial Revolution. This machine that allowed the urban settings to expand also took away something elemental. It devastated nature in a way that if it had continued, it could've eradicated life in the Canadian north. As easy as it seemed, the Canadian forest wasn't inexhaustible, and it was Grey Owl who opened people's eyes to this fact.

The Canadian government continued to provide housing to Grey Owl in Prince Albert National Park, just as it did to the beavers he raised and released into the park. It also supported efforts advocating for conservation. Beyond being Canada's most popular conservationist, Grey Owl did an incredible service to the country. He saved Canada's national animal from extinction, which, according to later environmental analysis, was imminent at the rate at which beaver country was disappearing.

Grey Owls warnings were heeded, and conservation efforts slowly replaced exploitation all across Canada. His success allowed not only his favorite animal, the beaver, to survive but also the Canadian wilderness and the Native People who inhabited it to sustain and thrive.

Grey Owl saved his favorite animal, the beaver, from extinction.

Grey Owl's publication and tours in Britain also played a part in his legacy. From the second half of the 18th century, Britain was one of the largest importers of beaver pelts on the European market. Due to the efforts of their own countryman with a made-believe First Nation persona, the English started to realize the true costs of their beautiful, imported fur. Soon, the previously insatiable market was experiencing a lull, making trapping and exporting beaver fur from Canada far less profitable.

According to his own words, Grey Owl grew increasingly passionate about creating a better future for everyone in the country:

"Every word I write, every lecture I have given, or ever will give, were and are to be for the betterment of the Beaver people, all wildlife, the Indians and half breeds, and for Canada, in whatever small way I may."

His work as a conservationist may have faded into the background when the truth of his origins was revealed, but his efforts made a difference. His legacy lives on as the beavers and the rest of the wildlife were made to thrive in the newly-grown and populated forests in the previously devastated areas. Indigenous people of Canada would continue to run into trouble trying to conserve their homelands, but they would always find inspiration in the works of conservationists like Grey Owl.

Chapter 5: Sir Arthur Currie and Agnes Macphail's Legacy

People who shaped Canadian history come in many forms, including an educator turned military leader and a farm-lover who rose to prominence in politics. This chapter discusses the distinctive contributions of Sir Arthur Currie and Agnes Macphail through military leadership and political advocacy, respectively, highlighting how their personal experiences and beliefs paved the path for their passion for making a difference.

Sir Arthur Currie.
https://commons.wikimedia.org/wiki/File:William_Orpen_-_Sir_Arthur_Currie.jpg

Sir Arthur Currie's Rise to Prominence

Arthur Currie was born to Irish immigrant parents in 1875 in Strathroy, Canada. After attending the local elementary school, he received an education to become a school teacher, but he chose to pursue other ventures. When Currie was 19, he moved to Victoria, British Columbia, and worked as an insurance agent, a real estate developer, and a manager in an insurance company. Fueled by a strong wish to contribute to his country, Currie also entered the militia, where he advanced to the Lieutenant Colonel rank by 1909. This experience in the militia led him down the path that saw him achieve several Canadian victories during World War I, including the one at the Battle of Vimy Ridge.

While serving in the Canadian militia, Arthur Currie befriended Garnet Hughes, a junior officer and son of the Minister of Militia and Defense, Samuel Hughes. While reluctant to offer a position in a Canadian Expeditionary Force to someone with no professional military experience, Samuel Hughes was ultimately convinced by his son to make Currie the commander of the 2nd Canadian Infantry Brigade. This decision would prove to be one of the best ones made during Canada's participation in World War I.

Tactical Genius

Currie and the Canadian troops arrived in England in the autumn of 1914 and spent the winter training under British general E.A.H. Aldersons command. Early the next year, they had their baptism by fire at the Second Battle of Ypres, where they also faced the unusual weapon used by the Germans, chlorine gas.

Despite suffering heavy losses, Currie was praised for his quick-thinking skills and was promoted to the commander of the 1st Canadian Division in September 1915. From May of the next year, the Canadian Corps was under the command of Sir Julian Byng, who saw a great ally in Commander Currie. While he wasn't a charismatic or particularly outspoken leader, Currie was a brilliant tactician, and Byng learned to take advantage of this. In June 1916, Currie was sent to strike a counterattack against the Nazi troops at Mount Sorrel, which he successfully executed. While his men suffered another monumental loss at the Battle of the Somme, they would prove their courage once again at the Battle of Vimy Ridge in April 1917.

Sir Julian Byng orchestrated the initial scheme of the Canadian attack at Vimy Ridge, but Arthur Currie's masterful execution was the true victory.

By this time, British and French forces were depleted from years of fighting and struggling to find new recruits, so they couldn't afford to spend more time watching how the stalemate would play out. They devised an offensive strategy in which the French troops would attack the Germans from the Aisne River in France while the British would create a diversion to pin down Nazi forces at Arras. The Canadian troops, as part of the British force, had the task to capture Vimy Ridge, a 5.6-mile-long rising amid the open countryside north of Arras, and gain a valuable strategic point for overseeing enemy positions on the east. According to the Canadian records: *"More of the war could be seen from atop Vimy Ridge than from any other place in France."*

After moving into the Vimy area, the Canadian army encountered a battlefield with remainders of the previous battles. Their first assignment was to restore and rebuild the half-destroyed and neglected trenches while seeking shelter in nearby homes and villages. The soldiers who couldn't be billeted in houses lived in tents and ancient underground caverns, which provided protection. They also hauled massive amounts of food, ammunition, and supplies to the front line, preparing for a hard battle. Roads were restored, and tramways were built to facilitate the movement of soldiers and supplies further. Naturally, this was done under the darkness of night to avoid the watchful eyes of the enemy. Meanwhile, the Canadians also executed small raiders across the German lines, often capturing prisoners, seizing goods, gathering intelligence, and doing anything else they could to rattle the enemy.

Part of Byng's and Currie's tactics was to build 11 tunnels, which allowed their troops to get to the front line safely without open exposure to the enemy lines. They even installed lighting, first-aid stations, water supplies, and chambers for headquarters in these tunnels. Another part of the scheme was to divide the remaining troops into four and, after assuming a side-by-side formation, attack on the slopes. While those who would emerge on the front line assumed their positions in front of the German lines, the other soldiers would move and deliver timed assaults on the open field, where other allied armies supported them.

They marked their own and the enemy's trench positions on the ground with tape and provided detailed information to the soldiers about the German army's strong points. As a revolutionary measure, maps, aerial photographs, and models conveyed all the relevant information and ensured victory.

Learning from their loss at the battle of Somme, the Canadian troops, led by Arthur Currie, also implemented other innovations. For example, they placed the command on a lower level on the battlefield. Currie also encouraged his soldiers to apply critical thinking and take initiative when needed. In other words, they should stop relying on military tactics they were taught beforehand. According to the records, another piece of advice he gave them was:

"Follow your lieutenant — and if he goes down, follow your corporal; prepare to outflank enemy machine gunners who might survive the initial artillery barrage and follow up with bayonets. Don't lose contact with the platoon next to you."

Moreover, variety was introduced among the infantry soldiers. Whereas, before, riflemen were considered the most efficient among these ranks, now other soldiers with specialized tasks like grenade throwing or machine gun operating would also become members of the infantry. The latter was accompanied by engineering troops in large waves, helping them erect defenses or overcome obstacles as they advanced toward the enemy lines.

The artillery played a crucial role in the assault as they were provided with a nearly unlimited supply of shells and shell fuses that would explode when coming in contact with a bomb rather than falling uselessly to the ground. The attackers' leading wave would move behind the protective shield of the allied fire. This made the enemy troops remain sheltered in their bunkers, unable to return the attack, while helping the Canadians advance until they were at the German trenches.

The artillery began the attack, and as described in the Official History of the Canadian Army in the First World War: "a crushing bombardment fell on the German positions. One Canadian observer records that the shells poured 'over our heads like water from a hose, thousands and thousands a day."

After four days of bombardment, the main attack took place. Just as with most of the preparation, Curry's attack was executed during the night, surprising the enemy at dawn. While it made advancing on the ridge harder, it also obscured the Canadians, who opened the attack behind the safety of the artillery barrage. They swept over the German trenches and emerged victorious from the battle. Despite thousands of lives lost on the Canadian side, the maneuver was successful. Without Curry's outstanding tactics, many more lives could have been lost, and the victory could have been lost as well.

After the battle, Byng became commander in the British armies and recommended Arthur Currie as his replacement as the commander of the Canadian Corps. Currie was given this position (becoming the first Canadian to do so) and was knighted. He soon obtained another difficult victory at Hill 70 and executed a masterfully-planned attack at Passchendaele. The attack consisted of four phases and was delivered in a two-week period. Currie also showcased his extraordinary planning and leadership skills at the Hundred Days Campaign, which marked the last Allied efforts in Germany's defeat and the end of World War I.

After the war, Currie's reputation was surrounded by many controversies, and for a while, his efforts in wartime were seemingly forgotten. While Prime Minister Borden acknowledged Currie's brilliance, Currie still faced heavy criticism for his actions on the final days. Namely, despite the overall victory, tens of thousands of lives were lost, making it look like Currie needlessly sacrificed Canadian soldiers.

From August 1919, Arthur Currie worked as a general inspector of the Canadian militia forces. He left this position in May of the next year when he was appointed principal and vice-chancellor of McGill University. Here, he again showed his tactical genius by becoming a vastly successful university administrator — a particularly surprising feat for someone who lacked post-secondary education himself.

Arthur Currie died in November 1933, but his legacy lives on. He is forever remembered for his mastery of challenging situations and attention to detail, even when time was of the essence on the battlefield.

Agnes Macphail's Journey to the Canadian House of Commons

Born in 1890 in Dundalk, Canada, Agnes Macphail was one of the many children in a farming family of Scottish origins. Hailing from a line of Scottish settlers populating Grey County in the 1800s, the family started their lives in a modest log house. In her letters to her friends later in life, Agnes recalls living in a dark and cold house during early childhood but loving it at the same time.

Agnes Macphail.

She and her siblings loved playing in the big kitchen, the heart of the home that was always warm, if from nothing else, from laughter. Later on, her family moved to a farm just outside Ceylon — and that is where one of Agnes' passions was born. Despising housework, which was considered a strictly feminine role, Agnes preferred to spend her days outside on the stony ground tilled for grazing livestock.

She liked breathing in the fresh air and the fragrance of the nearby conifers, but more than anything, she loved helping her father tend to the animals. Fortunately, her family had no objections to this, often encouraging her to put farm work in front of her schooling. According to Agnes, while there weren't many displays of affection in her family, they showed deep respect for each other. Everyone showed respect for other people's feelings and wishes, which she considered a far more powerful display of love.

Still, as Agnes loved school just as much as she did farm life, she fought hard to obtain permission to continue her education. In 1906, she entered Owen Sound Collegiate School, and two years later, realizing that she wanted to share her love for learning with others, she attended the Normal School for Teachers in Stratford, Ontario. After graduating in 1910, Agnes taught in several schools in Ontario and Alberta.

While she gained experience as a teacher, Agnes also became a regular attendee of social gatherings where women talked about domestic issues while men discussed politics. With her mind already set on avoiding marriage, these discussions persuaded Agnes to make a difference in all the issues she heard about. Rather than dedicating her life to creating a family and raising children, she chose the freedom that allowed her to make significant contributions to society instead.

Entering the Political Scene

While working at Pegg's School near Sharon, Ontario, Agnes Macphail joined local farming organizations, which allowed her to become a participating member of the agricultural cooperative movement. She also joined the United Farmers of Ontario (UFO), an organization that focuses on educating farmers on social and political matters. After becoming affiliated with the Progressive Party and emerging victorious in the 1919 Ontario provincial election, the UFO decided to nominate a representative in the House of Commons. Seeing her passion for making a difference, they choose Agnes Macphail, marking the beginning of her career in politics.

Her entrance to the political scene was also significant because, in Ontario, women had just obtained the right to vote in the Canadian government. In 1921, Agnes Macphail was the only female member of Parliament, and she gained just as much criticism as she had allies. Some argued that she could use her natural feminine charm to gain sympathy, while others criticized her for being an unmarried woman. Still, she fought to tackle political and social issues ranging from giving recognition and rights to farmers, helping people deal with the repercussions of World War I, and advocating for women's rights, prison reforms, and peace.

Hailing from a farming community, Agnes knew and spoke openly about the issues affecting those living in rural settings. Her election into the House of Commons was met with some protest at first (on account of being a woman), but she soon justified the confidence put in her. She fought for the farmer's equal treatment and refused to back down to "return to teaching in a small rural school" as members of the opposition claimed she should.

She also became a veritable champion for the working class. One of her major contributions was gaining better conditions for miners in eastern Canada. After openly criticizing the government for providing financial support to the British Empire Steel Corporation while leaving the miners with poor working conditions, she was able to obtain better wages for the miners. Immigrants and those working in rural environments also found an ally in Agnes Macphail. For example, she eradicated high tariffs benefiting manufacturers while putting farmers at a disadvantage. As a result, farmers were able to make a better living and were not pushed down by large companies. By promoting the cooperative movement, she also ensured that the interests of industrial workers and farmers remained protected. In 1924, she left the Progressive Party, and along with her Alberta colleagues, she formed the independent Ginger Group. This seemingly small group would become one of people's greatest allies during the Great Depression in the 1930s. Allying with other socialist, labor, and agrarian groups, the Ginger Group formed the Co-operative Commonwealth Federation (CCF), the entity that supported industry nationalization, fought for the welfare state, and provided uniform unemployment and health insurance, as well as pensions. While forced to leave the CCF in 1934, Agnes Macphail maintained contact with the organization and later rejoined, representing the party in the Ontario legislature in the 1940s.

Another one of Macphail's greatest accomplishments was her role in bringing on new prison reforms. Upon hearing about a riot at the Kingston Penitentiary, she decided to investigate the cause rather than delivering punishments and pushing everything under the rug, as the prison authorities usually dealt with similar situations. After learning about the deplorable conditions prisoners lived in, she knew that the Canadian penal system had to change. Part of this reform was providing education for prisoners who could be reformed. She also argued that instead of corporal punishment, prisoners should be given work to do, along with time for exercise and being outdoors, which could contribute to their mental and physical health. Agnes also pushed for more qualified wardens and medical personnel to be employed in prisons and for prisoners to have access to psychological counseling. Although most of her efforts were rebutted until 1935, when the Liberal Party replaced the Conservative government, the power heeded her advice. It founded the Royal Commission, which investigated the Penal System of Canada in-depth, and in 1939, began introducing 88 changes into the organization.

Being a pacifist, it's not surprising that Agnes Macphail advocated for peace during her entire political career. Besides becoming a member of the Women's International League for Peace and Freedom, she also held discussions at anti-war rallies. When learning that part of the official National Defense strategy was to finance the training of more soldiers, she argued against it, claiming it would only prolong the war. Instead, she proposed that the government should subsidize the physical and peace education of the youth, teaching them about the benefits of conflict resolution rather than how to defend themselves when conflicts arise.

In 1929, when she became the first female Canadian delegate to the League of Nations, she refused to take her pre-assigned seat on the Health and Welfare of Women and Children Committee. She chose to serve on the Disarmament Committee, knowing that position enabled her to make more meaningful changes. When World War II broke out, she reluctantly voted for Canada to join the war, considering that not aiding the Allies in defeating Hitler and the Nazi army would bring larger consequences than the war itself.

Agnes Macphail established the Elizabeth Fry Society of Canada, an organization that provided aid for women in conflict with the law. A feminist herself, Agnes nurtured a strong friendship with and drew inspiration from the works of Thérèse Casgrain and suffragist Nellie McClung. Besides supporting the Famous Five, who advocated for women's rights to become members of the Senate (by being officially and legally recognized as "Persons"), Agnes also advocated for gender equity. She wanted to eradicate legal, social, and professional discrimination against women. One of her major contributions on this front was opening discussions about modifying grounds for divorce.

Thérèse Casgrain.

After losing her seat at the House of Commons in 1943, Agnes made a living by holding lectures across Canada and the United States, writing campaigns for the Ontario CCF, and crafting articles for the Globe and Mail. However, after emerging victorious at a provincial election in York East, in Toronto, she became a member of the Ontario Legislature. Here, she continued advocating for women's rights, along with supporting farmers, prison inmates, and industrial workers.

As her final political victory, Agnes Macphail succeeded in passing Ontario's first equal pay legislation in 1951. The Female Employees Fair Remuneration Act was a monumental step toward equity in legislation. Shortly after, she lost her seat in the provincial elections but continued her work, crafting a detailed report on women's status in Ontario. Had she not succumbed to a debilitating illness in 1954, she would have been appointed to the Senate, where she would have continued to make a difference in Canada's political scene.

Although she was long portrayed in public as a strict, matronly woman, Agnes Macphail's legacy speaks volumes of her passionate and caring nature. She regretted having made the impression of a humorless and loveless person, but she never lamented fighting for what she thought was fair and just.

By refusing to remain in the place society dictated for her, she showed everyone just how much the power of dedication counts. Her stubbornness paid off, and her efforts have been commemorated in many ways ever since. From naming landmarks after her to displaying her personal possessions to establishing the Agnes Macphail Recognition Committee, there is no shortage of ways to remember her. More importantly, her time in the Parliament resulted in many changes, with effects still felt in modern times.

Chapter 6: James Wolfe, Louis-Joseph de Montcalm, and the Battle for Quebec

The Battle of Quebec (or the Battle of the Plains of Abraham) put global civilization on a new trajectory. European expansion created territorial disputes around the world, and the outcomes of these conflicts built modern society. The events that followed the battle reshaped Europe, America, and Canada, creating unique national identities as a byproduct of the European colonial age.

James Wolfe.
https://commons.wikimedia.org/wiki/File:James_Wolfe.jpeg

James Wolfe and Louis-Joseph de Montcalm revolutionized warfare. The clash of these military geniuses decided the fate of North America. Poetically, both men met their end in their final battle as they succumbed to wounds inflicted during the conflict. Wolfe emerged victorious, solidifying British control over Quebec. The French loss in Canada may have resulted in their support of the American Revolution.

Canada has been under French and British rule for different periods in its history. Today, Canada is a constitutional monarchy, which means that the King is the Head of State but entrusts power to the government to make decisions in the people's interests. Canada's transition from a French colony to its independent nation-state today is directly linked to the Battle of Quebec.

The outcomes of this battle also influenced the United States and set it on its journey toward becoming a global superpower. Without the Battle of Quebec, the American Revolution may not have been successful. The conflict between expansionist France and Britain drew lines that would guide humanity's destiny for centuries to come. This battle shows how colonialism shrunk the world and set the foundations of the globalized systems that society relies on today.

Magic lives in the finer details. James Wolfe and Louis-Joseph de Montcalm's isolated decisions echoed throughout the world and into the future. They never got to see the world they helped create, but in death, they helped birth a radically different Canada.

James Wolfe

James Wolfe is remembered as a Canadian hero. His memory reminds us to pursue our goals against the odds. His military precision and commitment to his cause led him to victory. Wolfe faced many struggles that overlapped with the peak of his military achievement. His familial disputes and health issues always burdened the capable leader. Despite his suffering and tragic end, Wolfe stuck to his values, giving his life for the cause he believed in.

Wolfe's commitment to the military and obsession with strategy lived on after his death. He posthumously published a training manual called "Instructions to Young Officers." This book was formed from his meticulous notes and included tactical advice and training methods.

Early Life

James Wolfe was born in 1727. His military father, Lieutenant-General Edward Wolfe, may have influenced his decision to join the army. Wolfe joined when he was only 14 years old. It was expected that Wolfe would follow in his highly respected father's footsteps. As an upper-middle-class family, upholding a legacy was essential.

With this pressure on his shoulders, Wolfe was dedicated to making a lasting impact in his military career. He was committed to carrying the torch from his decorated father and fighting for the country he loved. His hard work and loyalty quickly gained the attention of higher ranks. This propelled Wolfe's career until he reached the rank of Major-General. Wolfe's military career peaked with his victory over the French, which united the British colonies in North America, but his death never allowed him to enjoy the fruits of his labor. Wolfe's legend grew in death as he became one of the most influential military heroes in Canada.

Wolfe's military reputation was solidified, but his family life was tumultuous. The military hero wanted to get married to a woman he was head over heels in love with named Elizabeth Lawson. His mother rejected the marriage; however, he remained determined and found another young lady, Katharine Lowther, whom his mother again rejected. This broke down their relationship, and Wolfe never spoke to his mother again. The death of his brother further distanced him from his family.

Rise Through the British Ranks

After joining the military at the tender age of 14, Wolfe was quickly awakened to the harsh realities of war. Before he could reach his 18th birthday, Wolfe was on the frontlines at the Battle of Dettingen in 1743. The Duke of Cumberland was impressed with the young soldier's bravery, sense of duty, and intelligence, so he supported him in his early career. The Duke often advocated for Wolfe and would mention his name when opportunities arose.

A few years later, Wolfe fought in Culloden in 1746. He later served in Ireland and Scotland during the 1750s. During this period, James Wolfe grew in experience and started developing a tactical military mind with his accumulated knowledge. Wolfe continued to excel at various battles during the Seven Years' War, proving himself a valiant leader. He became a major general because of the skill he showed at the siege of Louisbourg in 1758.

Military Philosophies

James Wolfe was the ultimate military strategist. He obsessed with finding more efficient and effective ways of conducting warfare. He analyzed every aspect of battle, including strategic formations as well as equipment use. Wolfe was respected by those who served under him because of the high standards he demanded of them and himself. Wolfe focused on teamwork and unity, realizing that every person in a unit should be able to fully rely on one another in the life-and-death context of war. Therefore, Wolfe carried the same amount of equipment as his infantrymen, even though an officer was not required to do so.

Wolfe never married. The military became his main focus, which is likely why he excelled at it to the level he did. His singular focus on the goal of strengthening Britain made him one of the military's most valuable assets. Wolfe idealistically believed in the values of the army and embodied the soldier's identity to his core. Despite his health issues, Wolfe remained energetic, always looking to take on more responsibility. His life and victory inspired many artworks and monuments in British Canada.

Louis-Joseph de Montcalm

Although Wolfe emerged victorious on the other side of the conflict, his formidable opponent was Louis-Joseph de Montcalm. The two men respected each other as stories of their greatness spread. The last communication both men sent was to one another, but neither of the messages reached their destination because they both died before they could be delivered.

Louis-Joseph de Montcalm.
À venir., CC0, via Wikimedia Commons.
https://commons.wikimedia.org/wiki/File:Unknown_Artist,_Louis-Joseph,_Marquis_de_Montcalm_(mid-19_century)_001.jpg

Early Life

Like Wolfe, De Montcalm was born to a respected family. He came from nobility and was born in 1712 in Vestric-et-Candiac, France. De Montcalm enlisted in the army when he was 9. His family's wealth gave him a privileged position. De Montcalm's father purchased a captain's commission, which was a British military practice between the 17th and 19th centuries that allowed officer positions to *be bought.*

In 1735, De Montcalm's father died. Following his death, De Montcalm took over his father's title as the Marquis de Saint-Veran. He married Angelique Louise Talon du Boulay shortly after, and they remained a committed couple. As the Marquis de Saint-Veran, De Montcalm had power, but he inherited the debts that came with the position. His marriage to Angelique Louise Talon du Boulay helped improve his finances. Their marriage of convenience transformed into one of love as they went on to have many children.

The Mighty French Commander

Although he came from a wealthy family, De Montcalm's commitment to proving his worth in the military could not be overlooked. He quickly ascended the ranks because of his bravery and strategic excellence. His military career began in the War of Polish Succession when he participated in the sieges of Kehl and Philippsburg. He then fought in the siege of Prague during the War of Austrian Succession.

His valiant efforts were recognized, and De Montcalm was promoted to colonel in 1743. He was awarded the prestigious decoration of the Order of Saint Louis for his work in multiple Italian campaigns. De Montcalm went through one of the most horrific experiences of his short life. The strategist was captured in the Battle of Piacenza and suffered under the brutal conditions of an 18th-century war prison. Upon his release, De Montcalm was promoted to brigadier general and loyally served in the position until the end of the war in 1748.

King Louis XV then sent him to North America to apply his experience in the French and Indian War. De Montcalm exploded onto the battlefield, quickly becoming a boogeyman for the British troops. With a collective of French soldiers, Canadian militias, and Native American collaborators, De Montcalm captured Fort Oswego from the British. He continued his campaign and captured additional forts south of Lake Champlain. The British troops surrendered, and he negotiated peaceful terms, but the Native American soldiers attacked the released troops, killing 200 of them.

De Montcalm's final moment in the light was his last victory at the Battle of Fort Carillon. General James Abercrombie led 15,000 British soldiers against De Montcalm's much smaller force. De Montcalm's incredible military planning and Abercrombie's blunders led to a decisive victory. This would be the last time De Montcalm tasted success. The French leadership began pulling back resources in the Americas, while the British simultaneously invested more in their war effort.

The Battle of Quebec

A country's destiny can change in a moment. The Battle of the Plains of Abraham lasted less than an hour, but in that short time, the future of the Americas was shifted. In this dramatic victory, British dominance in North America was sealed. French natives still lived in Canada, which is why the country still has a large French-speaking population today. The constant clashes between France and Britain heated up into a full-blown conflict.

In 1756, the Seven Years' War (or the French and Indian War) commenced. The battles between Britain and France had now left the shores of Europe and were extending into one of the first global conflicts. The war was fought on multiple fronts, with European powers aligning to opposing sides of the conflict. The bulk of the fighting took place in Europe and in the Americas. The Battle of Quebec happened during the Seven Years' War, but the arena was getting set before this.

In the early 1750s, France expanded the colony into the Ohio River valley. This position was close to Britain, so they regularly clashed. Even when there was still official peace between the British and French governments, troops were already being sent to fight in the Americas. When the war started in 1756, the French had the upper hand. Under the leadership of Louis-Joseph de Montcalm, Britain suffered many losses. Realizing the benefits of imperialism, British Prime Minister William Pitt went on a fundraising campaign to ensure Britain's victory by borrowing all that he could. Britain had 13 colonies dispersed across North America. Their dispute with France was in the Isle of Orleans. The New France colony included Canada's great lakes and stretched to Louisiana and Mississippi.

Their ongoing frontier battles came to a crescendo at the Plains of Abraham. Although De Montcalm was riding high from his chain of victories, he was no match for the strategic genius of Wolfe. The major general sailed along the St. Lawrence River, docking in the southwest of Quebec. He then led 4,500 troops up the Heights of Abraham. They had the higher ground on the French army and fired down at them. Wolfe instructed his soldiers to double-load their muskets so that the volume could further disorient the French soldiers who were caught off guard.

Wolfe could not appreciate the swift victory because of the injuries he sustained and his death shortly after. He learned that he had won just before passing, allowing him to send a final letter to De Montcalm to negotiate terms of surrender. De Montcalm was injured as rifle fire ripped through his back. He died the next day, also attempting to establish communication with Wolfe.

France was devastated by the loss. Their military and imperial campaign in North America swiftly ended. Within a year, they lost all power in the region, and their influence in Europe was dwindling as well. The rebuilding process after the war took time, and they never endeavored to reclaim Canada from the British. Their assistance from America may have been motivated by plans to extend across the border, as the colonialists had no desire to move into Quebec.

The Leadership of the Generals

Both generals had hands-on leadership styles, throwing themselves into the most heated parts of battles and leading their troops from the front. Their young entry into their respective militaries gave them an edge by submerging them into the deep end so they could gain experience fast. They were ideologically driven, with Wolfe coming from an upper-middle-class family and De Montcalm from the nobility.

The generals gave their lives for their countries. They both fought for imperialist forces and were dedicated to fulfilling the expansionist dreams of their rulers. France and Britain are proud nations that constantly were at war. This attitude shone through on both sides of the Seven Years' War. The battle of Quebec was an almost miraculous deciding factor in the destiny of Canada. After De Montcalm was taken by surprise, he panicked and made irrational decisions, sending many of his men to their deaths. The outmaneuvering that Wolfe achieved is even more impressive when you consider De Montcalm's extensive war resume.

The Battle's Aftermath

When the dust of war settled, Canada was then firmly under British control. Not only did the French lose the Americas, but they were defeated across the globe by Britain, including in regions like India. France did not forget the humiliation Britain inflicted on them, as they later funded the Colonists against the Loyalists. However, the French citizens in Canada had no desire to retake the territory, especially considering they lacked weapons, organization, and funding.

Britain would later bear the consequences of the expensive war. Like the French, which eventually lost control of Canada, the United States gained independence by seceding from the empire. The unforeseen outcomes of the war redefined Europe and the Americas. The Battle of Quebec paved the way for the transition out of the colonial age and the birth of independent nation-states in the Americas and globally.

Turning Point in Canadian History

Canada always swung between British and French rule. The outcomes of the Battle of Quebec firmly installed Britain as the European power controlling North America. The battle occurred in 1759, and by 1760, all the French forces were kicked out of the country. Following their humiliating defeat, the Treaty of Paris was signed. In the agreement, all of France's claims on Canadian territory were lost, and Britain claimed many French holdings in various countries. Additionally, Louisiana was given to Spain, while Britain controlled Spanish Florida and Upper Canada.

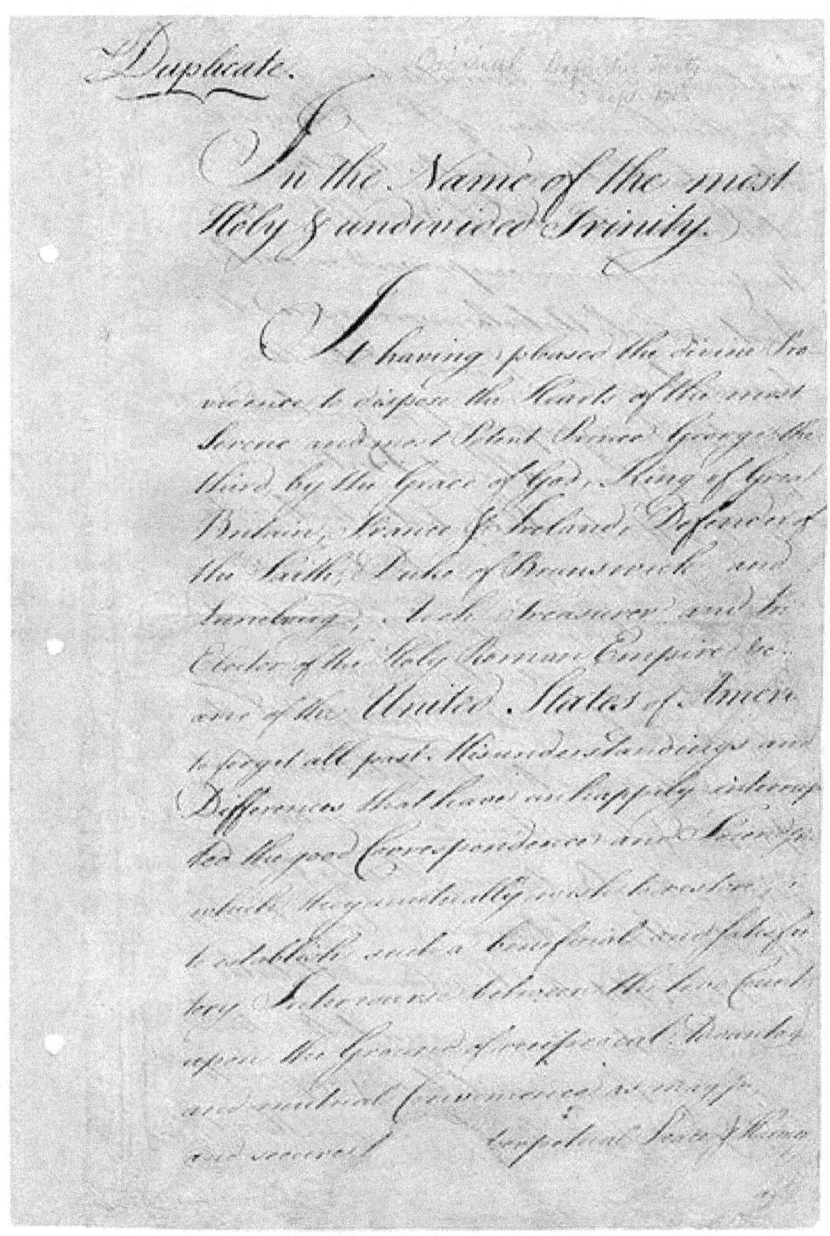

The first page of the Treaty of Paris.
https://commons.wikimedia.org/wiki/File:Treaty_of_Paris_(1783).jpg

The victory strengthened the 13 colonies. The power of the colonies prompted the Crown to exercise more control over the region. The Colonialists were becoming accustomed to living in relative freedom, distant from the influence of British officials. The increased control and imposition of high taxes resulted in the American Revolution, during which the country won its independence as a nation-state.

Canada remained loyal to the Crown but chose not to intervene in the American conflict. Fears that the French would reclaim control of Canada spread, but even French Canadians did not have the political will to stand against British rule. The small British colony focused on domestic issues. Although the Seven Years' War contributed to the American Revolution, the action remained relatively distant from Canada. This distance allowed Canada to continue functioning as a colony, leading to the constitutional monarchy the country enjoys now.

Geopolitics of the Region

The discovery of the New World reinvigorated the imperialist drives of European nations. Everyone was looking to stake a claim to these fruitful lands, which resulted in many disputes. Spain and Portugal initiated the expansion into the Americas, but eventually, Britain and France got into the game. North America presented an opportunity to increase the power of an empire through commercial means.

With each country staking claim to different parts of the land, their frontier borders became hotbeds for conflict. Amid colonial struggles, battles in Europe broke out regularly, with different kingdoms allying with various superpowers, such as France and Britain. The war was global, with disputed regions across the planet. Imperialism's motivations attracted European nations to the far reaches of the planet. The gold rush of colonialism birthed war because the spoils of conquering were clear as nations grew in resources and influence.

The funds that Britain borrowed to fight against the French in America had unforeseen knock-on effects. The war was expensive, putting Britain in an uncomfortable financial position. This is why they raised taxes in the colonies, which was a large contributor to the motivation for the American Revolution. The limitations the Crown placed on Western expansion may have also built onto the growing dissatisfaction Colonialists had with the Crown.

The Battle's Impact on Modern Canada

Today, Canada has a large French-speaking population and is still under Britain. The amalgamation of these two cultures is sown into the Canadian identity. The impact of the Battle of Quebec extended beyond the confines of Canada. The Seven Years' War was a global conflict involving many European components and Native American contributions.

Expelling the French to increase Britain's dominance eventually led to the development of American and Canadian identities separate from European rule. The defeat of the French in Canada fueled the vitriol against Britain, which led to their support of the American Revolution.

The U.S., Canada, and Britain are global allies today. The U.S. has risen to a superpower, and Canada has close ties to the country. The early conflicts when organizing the Americas resulted in much bloodshed and turmoil. It took centuries before there was true stability in North America. How Canada and the United States look today are far from the conditions of the chaotic past. Without the sacrifice of brave people and the dedication to create a new world, the inspiring freedom and human rights enjoyed in Canada may not have existed.

Chapter 7: Alexander Graham Bell and the Spirit of Invention

Alexander Graham Bell is a name not just known in Canada but throughout the whole world, for he brought the telephone into existence. Not just that, he was also responsible for incredible contributions to the deaf community. Bell's work changed not just how people communicate today but so much more. He paved the way for technology as you know it today, laying the foundation for a world where anything seems possible. There's so much more to his story, especially when it comes to his journey in Canada. So, keep reading and find out about the extraordinary life and legacy of Alexander Graham Bell.

Alexander Graham Bell.
https://commons.wikimedia.org/wiki/File:Alexander_Graham_Bell.jpeg

Early Life

On a chilly day in March 1847, in the heart of Edinburgh, Scotland, the Bell family welcomed a new addition. This little bundle of joy was none other than Alexander, named after both his grandfather and his father.

Now, Grandfather Bell, who lived in London, was quite the educator. He had a knack for helping children with speech trouble like stuttering. He delved deep into the secrets of spoken words, studying how our lungs, vocal cords, lips, and faces all play a role in talking. Alexander's father, Melville, followed in those footsteps, teaching speech himself, so naturally, they expected young Alexander to do the same.

However, here's the thing about little Aleck, as his family fondly called him – he was a curious soul. With his pale face, brown eyes, and bushy dark hair, he was always off on some adventure. Alongside his brothers, Melly and Ted, he'd roam the Scottish countryside, collecting all sorts of treasures, from plants to animal bones.

One fateful summer day in 1850, the Bells went on a picnic, and wouldn't you know it, curious Aleck wandered off to explore. He stumbled upon a wheat field that seemed to stretch forever. Sitting down among the swaying wheat, he closed his eyes and wondered if he could hear it growing, but alas, silence. Eventually, he tried to find his way back to the picnic, only to get lost in the towering wheat. It took his father's voice to guide him back to safety.

Aleck wasn't exactly a star student. Greek, Latin, math – they all bored him to tears, but plants, animals, and music? Now, that was more his speed. His mother, Eliza, taught him to play the piano despite being nearly deaf herself. Using a special ear tube, she felt the music's vibrations against the piano keys. Aleck had a special way of speaking to his mom, softly placing his mouth on her forehead so she could hear the vibrations of his words.

Eliza encouraged Aleck's curiosity and creativity, but his father did not do much. Melville had grand plans for his son to excel academically, often interrupting Aleck's piano lessons with dull discussions about science. Aleck was very independent and original. Inspired by a family friend, he chose to adopt a new middle name – Graham – and from that day forward, he became Alexander Graham Bell.

A Turning Point

In 1862, after completing high school, Aleck faced his father's concern over his lack of direction. The solution, as Melville saw it, was to send Aleck to live with his grandfather in London. Despite Aleck's reluctance to leave his mother and brothers, he found himself on a train bound for London, starting a journey that would alter his life's course.

London, bustling and sprawling, stood in stark contrast to Edinburgh's quaint charm. The world's largest city at the time, London had grand palaces, majestic cathedrals, bustling theaters, and the imposing Houses of Parliament, where government matters were deliberated. Aleck was taken aback by the sheer number of people and the city's polluted air, a far cry from the cleaner, quieter streets of Edinburgh.

Living with Grandfather Bell meant adhering to a strict set of rules, including dressing as a gentleman whenever stepping outside – a dark suit, stiff white shirt, tie, top hat, gloves, and a cane were mandatory attire. Aleck also had to be rigorous in his studies – six days a week, although many subjects failed to capture his interest. Yet, observing his grandfather's speech lessons ignited a spark within him. Given the freedom to explore London independently, Aleck gravitated toward the library, where he got interested in books on sound. Reflecting on this period later in life, he noted it as the turning point of his career.

Upon Melville's visit to London, they encountered the renowned inventor, Sir Charles Wheatstone, who showcased an invention – a speaking box – that captured their imagination. Inspired, Melville challenged Aleck and his brother, Melly, to create their own version. Working together, Melly crafted the "lungs" and "throat," while Aleck fashioned the "tongue" and "mouth," shaping them for clarity of speech. Their efforts resulted in the creation of a speaking machine, which they demonstrated at the bottom of their house's stairway. The lifelike voice it produced, uttering "Mamma, mamma," astonished their neighbors, who mistook it for a real infant's cry. This achievement was only the beginning of Aleck's journey toward inventing the telephone, which was spurred on by the challenge set by his father.

Exploring New Paths

At the age of sixteen, Aleck felt the urge to break free from home, perhaps to become a sailor. However, a newspaper advertisement altered his course. The Weston House Academy in Elgin needed teachers for music and speech. Both Aleck and his brother, Melly, secretly applied, listing their father as a reference. Initially angered by their actions, Melville eventually saw the opportunity and sent Melly to the University of Edinburgh while Aleck headed to Weston House Academy.

The University of Edinburgh.

In Elgin, Aleck found himself in a bustling city quite different from his hometown of Edinburgh. Despite the initial shock, he adapted to the new environment and thrived as a teacher, even though he was younger than some of his students. Upon his return home, he discovered his father had invented Visible Speech, a revolutionary method for teaching speech to the deaf.

Joined by his sons, Melville toured Scotland, demonstrating the effectiveness of Visible Speech. These demonstrations deepened Aleck's interest in speech and sound. He experimented with tuning forks, discovering similarities between speech and musical tones. Inspired by a German scientist's work, Aleck envisioned the possibility of transmitting voice sounds over telegraph wires.

The idea of a talking telegraph fascinated Aleck, reminiscent of Samuel Morse's invention of the telegraph in 1835. Morse's telegraph transmitted messages through electrical currents, which were converted into dots and dashes of Morse code, allowing communication across long distances.

Aleck's exploration into speech, sound, and telegraphy laid the groundwork for his future inventions. With a growing understanding of the connections between speech and technology, he embarked on a journey that would eventually lead to the invention of the telephone.

A New Beginning in Canada

On August 7, 1905, tragedy struck the Bell family with the passing of Grandfather Bell. This marked a turning point as Melville decided to relocate the family to London, intending to take over his father's business. However, sorrow struck once more when eighteen-year-old Ted Bell fell ill and succumbed to tuberculosis in May 1867. Three years later, Aleck's older brother, Melly, also lost his battle with the same disease.

The family was devastated, and Eliza and Melville grew fearful for Aleck's health, noticing his recent complaints of headaches. Seeking a change, they made a bold decision to move across the Atlantic to Canada, settling in Brantford, Ontario. The fresh air and beautiful surroundings helped Aleck recover, and he spent his time experimenting with sound.

In April 1871, Aleck made another move, this time to Boston, Massachusetts. He secured a teaching position at the renowned Boston School for the Deaf, where his patience and use of his father's Visible Speech system enabled many students to speak for the first time, astonishing their parents and attracting more students to the school.

Aleck also provided private lessons, including to five-year-old George Sanders, the deaf son of a wealthy businessman. Using a special glove with the alphabet, Aleck taught George to read and spell, opening up a world of communication for him and delighting his father.

Always seeking innovative ways to help people communicate, Aleck was intrigued by the Western Union Telegraph Company's ability to send two messages simultaneously over telegraph wires. This sparked an idea – what if he could send multiple sounds down telegraph wires simultaneously? Thus, the concept of a harmonic telegraph was born, and Aleck set out to make it a reality.

Fortune smiled upon him when he was offered a position at Boston University despite lacking a college degree. With a good salary, continued work with private students, and a dedicated space for his experiments, Aleck, now known as Alexander Graham Bell, embarked on a promising future at just twenty-six years old.

A New Direction

During the summer of 1874, Alexander Graham Bell found himself in Brantford, supposedly for rest, though he was anything but idle. Fascinated by a machine called the phonautograph, which translated sound waves into visual patterns, Aleck pondered the possibility of using sound waves to produce electric currents. This sparked the idea of transmitting spoken words across telegraph wires – a concept that would bring him closer to inventing the telephone.

Amid his inventive pursuits, Aleck's attention turned to sixteen-year-old Mabel Hubbard, one of his students from Boston. Deaf since childhood, Mabel could lip-read but struggled with speech clarity. Her parents, Gertrude and Gardiner Greene Hubbard, hoped Aleck could assist her. Initially unimpressed by Aleck's appearance and demeanor, Mabel's perception gradually shifted as her father recognized Aleck's potential to invent a new telegraph system.

Gardiner Hubbard's dissatisfaction with the Western Union Telegraph Company, the sole telegraph provider, prompted him to seek alternatives. Recognizing Aleck's ingenuity, he offered financial support to fuel his inventions. Meanwhile, another inventor, Elisha Gray, also vied for the title of telegraph innovator, setting the stage for a rivalry between Gray and Bell in their race to invent both the harmonic telegraph and the telephone.

The Birth of the Speaking Telephone

In 1874, Alexander Graham Bell, although supported by Thomas Sanders and Gardiner Greene Hubbard for his work on a new telegraph, remained unsatisfied. While the harmonic telegraph interested his backers, Aleck's true ambition lay in transmitting spoken words across wires. Seeking assistance, he enlisted the help of Thomas Watson, a skilled craftsman at the Charles Williams Electrical Supply Company.

Despite pressure from Hubbard and Sanders to focus solely on the harmonic telegraph, Aleck and Thomas embarked on their quest to create a telephone. They continued their day jobs but collaborated in the shop's attic at night. While working on the harmonic telegraph, Aleck shared his dream of inventing a telephone with Thomas.

However, Hubbard and Sanders were skeptical about the practicality of a device that transmitted voice over wires and urged Aleck to concentrate on the telegraph. Threatened with the withdrawal of financial support, Aleck faced a dilemma.

Meanwhile, Thomas Watson, born in Salem, Massachusetts, in 1854, found his passion for invention at Charles Williams's machine shop. It was there that he crossed paths with Alexander Graham Bell. The invention of the telephone later made Watson a wealthy man.

In June 1875, Aleck and Thomas experimented with using reeds to transmit sounds down electrical wires. When Thomas plucked a stuck reed, Aleck, holding the receiver in another room, heard a ping. This revelation confirmed that sound could indeed travel across wires. Excited by the discovery, Thomas remarked that the speaking telephone was born at that moment.

A picture of Bell on the phone.
https://commons.wikimedia.org/wiki/File:Alexander_Graham_Telephone_in_Newyork.jpg

The Race for the Telephone Patent

Excited by their discovery, Aleck began sketching potential designs for the telephone. However, he also felt guilty for dedicating so much time to this new invention. He wrote a letter to Mr. Hubbard explaining the significance of his accidental discovery.

Unfortunately, Mr. Hubbard remained unimpressed and even threatened to jeopardize Aleck's relationship with Mabel if he continued his pursuit of the telephone. Undeterred, Aleck wrote another letter to Hubbard, declaring that if Mabel couldn't accept him for who he was, then he didn't want her at all.

Fortunately, Mabel's love for Aleck was unwavering, and on her eighteenth birthday, she accepted his proposal. As a condition, she requested Aleck to drop the "k" in his nickname, henceforth known as Alec. They married on July 11, 1877.

Despite Mabel's pleas for Alec to ease his workload, the telephone consumed Alec's thoughts. With Thomas, he made gradual progress on a model. Alec spoke into a mouthpiece with a tight covering, which vibrated with his voice's sound waves, initiating an electrical current to reproduce voice sounds. However, clarity remained an issue.

Recognizing Alec's progress, Hubbard and Sanders urged him to secure a patent before others. Although Alec preferred to wait until the telephone improved, his partners were anxious.

On February 14, 1876, without Alec's knowledge, Hubbard and Sanders filed for the patent. Just two hours later, Elisha Gray attempted the same, believing his model superior. However, Gray's efforts were in vain. Alec had won the race to invent the telephone, securing the patent.

The Invention

On March 7, 1876, Alexander Graham Bell was granted U.S. patent number 174,465A for his telephone. Now, he and Thomas had the task of creating a functional one.

Just three days later, they achieved success. Working in their lab, Alec held a mouthpiece in one room while Thomas listened with a receiver pressed to his ear in another. Suddenly, Thomas heard Alec's voice saying, "Watson – come here – I want to see you!" It sounded urgent, but Alec was actually jubilant. Thomas had heard and understood Alec's words over the telephone wire!

In a letter to his father, Alec expressed his excitement, foreseeing a future where telephone wires would be as commonplace as water or gas lines.

1876 marked the United States' centennial year, celebrated with the Centennial Exposition in Philadelphia. Almost ten million visitors came to marvel at various exhibits, including art, food, and innovative gadgets. Mr. Hubbard urged Alec to showcase his telephone at the fair despite Alec's reluctance due to his commitments in Boston and reluctance to leave Mabel behind. Additionally, Elisha Gray, now holding a patent for the multiple telegraph, would be demonstrating his invention at the event.

Reluctantly, Alec agreed to attend and set up his telephone in a small corner of the convention hall. Initially unnoticed, Alec's invention caught the attention of Don Pedro II, the emperor of Brazil, who recognized Alec from a previous visit to the Boston School for the Deaf. Intrigued, the emperor and other judges approached Alec's exhibit. When one of them listened through the receiver and heard Alec's voice clearly, the excitement spread.

Don Pedro II enthusiastically declared his success, leading to Alec receiving the Gold Medal for Electrical Equipment. This recognition catapulted the telephone into the limelight, but Alec knew there was still much work to be done to improve its functionality over longer distances, so he returned to his work, as he always did.

The Telephone Takes Off

Alec and Thomas started giving lectures and demonstrations of their revolutionary invention. As Alec continued to refine his telephone, its capabilities expanded. Initially, they had to be in the same hall to demonstrate it, but soon, they could communicate from increasingly greater distances – two miles, eight miles, twenty miles, and eventually thirty-two miles, marking what were considered long-distance calls at the time.

While newspapers ran articles about the telephone, public interest didn't necessarily translate into sales. Mr. Hubbard proposed selling the rights to the telephone to Western Union for $100,000, but they declined, claiming to have other inventors working on similar projects, including Thomas Edison and Elisha Gray. Gray's involvement particularly troubled Bell, as rumors suggested he might have invented the telephone.

Fortunately, telephone orders began to trickle in as people recognized its potential to change their lives. On July 9, 1877, Alexander Graham Bell, Thomas Watson, Gardiner Greene Hubbard, and George Sanders established the Bell Telephone Company, anticipating substantial profits from their invention.

After their wedding, Alec and Mabel traveled to England, where Queen Victoria was impressed by the telephone's demonstration and promptly placed an order. Meanwhile, trouble brewed in the United States as Western Union established its own telephone company despite Alec holding the patent. Additionally, the Bell Company faced challenges in installing telephone wires, opting for telephone poles – a costly endeavor that required more investors, fortunately found in Boston businessmen like William H. Forbes.

Inventor to the End

Even after countless court battles defending his invention, Alexander Graham Bell faced over six hundred claims challenging his invention of the telephone. Yet, he emerged victorious each time, securing the legacy of the Bell Telephone Company and his own fortune. However, as success grew, so did Alec's weariness with the telephone business. Surprisingly, he even considered the telephone a nuisance, refusing to have one in his study.

By 1880, Alec sought to leave the company and move on to new endeavors. Settling in Washington, DC, he continued his quest to aid the hearing-impaired, developing the audiometer to test hearing abilities. His relentless pursuit of innovation led to inventions like the photophone, although not all achieved widespread acceptance.

In a moment of crisis, Alec's metal detector failed to locate a bullet in President Garfield's body, showcasing the limitations of early medical technology. Meanwhile, personal tragedy struck when Alec lost his newborn son, Edward, but he turned his grief into inspiration, inventing a breathing machine that laid the groundwork for the iron lung.

Seeking solace and space for experimentation, Alec relocated his family to Baddeck, Nova Scotia, where he built Beinn Bhreagh, a hub for scientific exploration. Engaging in kite experiments and exploring flight, Alec's contributions extended beyond telecommunication. His work with kites even influenced the design of the George Washington Bridge.

Determined to further scientific knowledge, Alec joined the National Geographic Society, eventually becoming its president and overseeing its expansion. His commitment to education extended to the deaf community, as seen in his influential meeting with Helen Keller, which paved the way for her remarkable journey as an activist and author.

Throughout his life, Alec saw himself not just as an inventor but as a teacher, finding fulfillment in his work's impact on education and communication. His legacy endures through his groundbreaking inventions, his contributions to the National Geographic Society, and his lasting influence on the lives of countless individuals, including the remarkable Helen Keller.

The End

Alexander Graham Bell was an inventor, teacher, husband, father, and friend. His guidance to students and children alike reflected his belief in charting one's own path, urging them to venture off the beaten track to discover new horizons.

Even after achieving wealth through his inventions, notably the telephone, Alec's insatiable curiosity kept him engaged in work, driven by a passion for exploration. The sign in his lab, bearing the words "Keep on fighting," epitomized his relentless pursuit of knowledge.

Despite advancing age and health challenges, including diabetes, Alec remained committed to his pursuits. On August 2, 1922, at the age of seventy-five, Alexander Graham Bell passed away with Mabel, his devoted wife, by his side. His funeral day marked a poignant moment as telephone service across the United States paused for a minute, honoring the man whose groundbreaking invention transformed communication and touched countless lives.

Chapter 8: Lucy Maud Montgomery's Literary Landscape

The literary world would have looked very different today without the novels of Lucy Maud Montgomery, Canada's most famous author. Lucy was a brilliant wordsmith who used vivid imagery that brought her stories to life. You could feel the characters' emotions and see the beautiful settings she described. They weren't just words on paper but people you sympathize with and places you long to visit. She used her sad childhood to create iconic characters and heartwarming stories that people read to this day.

Lucy Maud Montgomery.

This chapter tells Lucy's story and all the struggles and pain she lived through that made her one of the world's greatest authors.

Biography

Lucy Maud Montgomery was born on 30 November 1874 in Clifton, now New London. She came from a wealthy family. Her great-grandfather was the House of Assembly speaker, and her grandfather was a senator. However, she didn't have a happy childhood. Her mother, Clara Woolner Macneill Montgomery, died at the age of 23 when Lucy was two.

Lucy didn't remember her mother's smile or her kind touch. She only remembered her lying still in the coffin. The image haunted her throughout her life. She wrote about the experience in her autobiography, *The Alpine Path: The Story of My Career.*

> *"I did not feel any sorrow, for I knew nothing of what it all meant. I was only vaguely troubled. Why was Mother so still? And why was Father crying? I reached down and laid my baby hand against Mother's cheek. Even yet I can feel the coldness of that touch."*

Lucy's father was devastated after the loss of his beloved wife. He was too depressed to take care of Lucy, so he sent her to live with her maternal grandparents, Alexander and Lucy Woolner Macneil, in Cavendish on Prince Edward Island. Her father couldn't stay in Clifton and moved to Prince Albert, Saskatchewan. A few years later, he remarried and started a new family.

Lucy's grandparents were kind and gave her everything she needed, but she wasn't happy. She was lonely because there weren't other children her age to play with, so she decided to create her own world. Her imagination was her refuge. Inside her head, she could make friends and go on adventures.

At the age of six, Lucy started school. During this time, she discovered her passion for writing. She kept a journal where she recorded her thoughts and feelings at the age of nine. Writing was her therapy and her only escape.

She wrote in her journal, *"I cannot remember a time when I was not writing, or when I did not mean to be an author. To write has always been my central purpose around which every effort and hope and ambition of my life has grouped itself."*

She also began writing poetry at a young age. She published her first poem, *On Cape LeForce,* in 1890 in a newspaper called *The Daily Patriot"* at the age of 16. She used pen names such as Maud Cavendish or Joyce Cavendis to conceal her identity. Later, she used the name L.M. Montgomery so people wouldn't know that she was a female.

In 1890, Lucy visited her father and his new family. She was homesick and miserable and wanted to return to Prince Edward Island. Her father didn't pay much attention to her, and she felt like a stranger. She also didn't have a good relationship with her stepmother.

Lucy returned home to her maternal grandparents in 1891. She often visited her other grandparents and her extended family. However, none of them was affectionate or tried to be a parental figure to her. The more she grew, the more lonely and isolated she became. These feelings stayed with her for the rest of her life and were reflected in many of her writings.

> *"She had never before minded being alone. Now she dreaded it. When she was alone now she felt so dreadfully alone."* Anne's House of Dreams.

Lucy attended Prince of Wales College to earn her teacher's certificate. It was a two-year program, but Lucy was a clever and hard-working student. She graduated after one year with honors.

She began her teaching career, but in less than a year, she took a break to study English literature at Dalhousie University in Halifax, Nova Scotia. However, Lucy left college after one year because she didn't have enough money to continue her education and earn a degree.

Lucy returned to Prince Edward Island and her teaching job. Her life revolved around her work and her writing. She published multiple short stories and earned money. She began to feel more independent as her financial situation improved.

After her grandfather passed away, she moved back to Cavendish to live with her grandmother. During that time, she held many jobs. She was a proofreader for the Daily Echo, and she wrote a society column under the pen name *Cynthia*; people looked forward to it each week. She also published multiple stories and poems.

Romance

Lucy was an attractive and intelligent young woman who caught many young men's attention. She was involved in a few relationships, which inspired her work. During her late teens, she turned down a marriage proposal from a young boy named Nate Lockhart because she didn't reciprocate his feelings. When she was in college, her teacher, John Mustard, was in love with her, but she found him dull. Her friend, Laura's brother, Will Pritchard, also tried to win her heart, but she only cared for him as a friend. Their friendship continued until Will passed away in 1897.

At the age of 23, Lucy was worried that she would remain unmarried, so she accepted her distant cousin, Edwin Simpson's marriage proposal. However, soon after their engagement, she began to despise Edwin and fell in love with a young farmer named Herman Leard. She ended her engagement to Edwin, against her family's wishes, and followed her heart.

Lucy had a brief relationship with Herman until his death. She was heartbroken and vowed never to love again.

However, her feelings changed when she met a minister named Ewan Macdonald. The couple were secretly engaged in 1906 and married in 1911 after her grandmother died. They spent their honeymoon in England and Scotland.

Minister Ewan Macdonald.

After their honeymoon, they moved from Prince Edward Island to Ontario so Ewan would be near his parish. They had two sons, Chester and Stuart.

Lucy and Ewan had different personalities, and he wasn't interested in history or literature. However, Lucy was adamant about making her marriage work and giving her children the family life she never had. The couple eventually fell out of love, but they became good friends and lived a quiet life together.

After the First World War, Lucy's life turned upside down. She had the Spanish flu and was in bed for weeks – and nearly died. Her husband also suffered severe depression.

She also discovered that her publisher, L.C. Page, was stealing royalties from her Green Gables books. She sued him, and after a long and costly case, Lucy won the rights to her novels.

Lucy's life wasn't easy. Being a minister's wife and a mother was demanding. She didn't always have time to write. Ewan's depression also got worse, and he admitted himself to a sanatorium and resigned from his parish.

After he was released, he was prescribed multiple medications. One time, the drugstore made a mistake and put poison in his antidepressant medication, and he nearly died. Ewan was unstable and believed Lucy tried to kill him. That incident started Ewan's abusive behavior that she endured for years. Lucy also suffered from depression, and her husband's actions took a toll on her mental health.

Lucy loved her children dearly. Although writing was her passion, she believed motherhood was the world's most significant job. Her maternal duty and sadness for losing her mother were usually reflected in her work.

Literary Legacy

Lucy used her pain and struggles to create masterpieces that left a unique mark on Canadian literature. Although she had been dead for decades, she will remain immortal through her work.

Anne of Green Gables

One can't talk about Lucy Maud Montgomery without mentioning her first and most popular novel, *Anne of Green Gables*. It tells the story of 11-year-old Anne Shirley, an intelligent, mature, and passionate orphan who goes to live with elderly siblings Marilla and Matthew Cuthbert. However, they wanted a boy to work on their farm, Green Gable. The book follows Anne's adventures until adolescence and how she wins her new parents' hearts. The story is set in Prince Edward Island.

Lucy found inspiration for her novel in children's classics such as Alice in Wonderland and Little Women. She also read a newspaper story about a couple who arranged to adopt a boy, but the orphanage sent them a girl by mistake.

Lucy finished her story in 1905 and sent it to many publishers, but they all rejected it. She was discouraged and gave up until 1907 – the same year she met L.C. Page.

Anne of Green Gables was published in 1908 and was highly received by readers and critics. It sold over 19,000 copies in five months and was printed ten times in one year. It also garnered widespread acclaim in the literary world. Canadian poet Bliss Carman described Anne as "one of those flesh and blood characters whom we cherish in the quiet places of our hearts; kept for the dearest mortals we know." American author Mark Twain also said that Anne was "the dearest, most moving and delightful child since the immortal Alice." After the First World War, Lucy became one of the most famous authors worldwide.

Many critics and readers believe that Lucy is similar to Anne as both are orphans, both smart and spirited, and both are sent to live with a new family. Although Lucy understood why people drew this connection, she believed that she was more similar to Emily from *Emily of New Moon* than Anne.

> *"People were never right in saying I was Anne, but, in some respects, they will be right if they write me down as Emily."* An excerpt from a letter she sent to author Ephraim Weber in 1921.

After the great success *Anne of Green Gables* received and the popularity of her heroine, Lucy turned her story into a book series following Anne's journey to adulthood until she got married and had a child. The second book, *Anne of Avonlea* (1909), showed a mature, mellow, and more confident version of Anne, who became a teacher but struggled with her new job. Her young readers appreciated Anne's character development as they also grew up and wanted to experience adulthood with their favorite character.

The third book, *Anne of the Island* (1915), took Anne to college, where she began her love story with her future husband, Gilbert Blythe. The fourth book, *"Anne of Windy Poplars"* (1936), mainly consisted of Anne's letters to Gilbert.

The fifth book, *Anne's House of Dreams* (1917), focused on Anne and Gilbert as a married couple, their new life together, and the new friendships they formed. Anne also became a mother, which was a challenging but rewarding role.

The sixth book, *Anne of Ingleside* (1939), showed Anne pregnant with five kids. The seventh book, *Rainbow Valley* (1919), focused on Anne's children. The last book, *Rilla of Ingleside* (1921), tells the story of Anne's youngest daughter, Rilla.

The books weren't published in chronological order. The fourth book was the seventh published, while the sixth book was published eighth and was Lucy's last published work during her lifetime.

Anne and her children were featured in Lucy's other novels and short stories, such as *The Blythes are Quoted, Chronicles of Avonlea,* and *Further Chronicles of Avonlea.*

Emily of New Moon Trilogy

Emily of New Moon trilogy was another best-seller. Lucy's other beloved main character was similar to Anne. Emily was also an orphan and went to live with unmarried siblings. The novels followed her journey as she embarked on her new life until she came of age.

Emily was the character Lucy most identified with as she was also independent, wise, an avid reader, and a writer.

The Emily of New Moon trilogy.

Other Publications

In addition to her two popular book series, Lucy wrote six successful novels: *The Blue Castle* (1926), *Magic for Marigold* (1929), *A Tangled Web* (1931), *Pat of Silver Bush* (1933), *Mistress Pat* (1935), and *Jane of Lantern Hill* (1937).

During her lifetime, she wrote 20 novels, an autobiography, 500 poems, 30 essays, and 530 short stories. Although most people only know her as the woman behind Anne Shirley, Lucy's collected work shows her as a literary genius who was capable of creating complex characters and worlds.

Common Themes

Motherhood was the most common theme in Lucy's novels. She often portrayed her characters as orphans or separated from their parents and had to live with unaffectionate relatives, mirroring her own life. The theme was present from her first novel, *Anne of Green Gables*, to her last one, *Jane of Lantern Hill*, which showed how losing her mother and growing up without her parents affected her.

Nature was another common theme in Lucy's novels. Growing up in Prince Edward Island, a place famous for its natural scenery, influenced Lucy's writing. Her vivid descriptions of nature showed she had spent a long time outdoors observing the trees, mountains, oceans, etc. Nineteen of her twenty novels were set on Prince Edward Island, and her narrative focused on the beauty of its landscape.

Lucy's favorite part of her childhood was living in a home surrounded by trees. She spoke about it in her autobiography.

> *"I am grateful that my childhood was spent in a spot where there were many trees, trees of personality, planted and tended by hands long dead, bound up with everything of joy or sorrow that visited our lives. When I have 'lived with' a tree for many years it seems to me like a beloved human companion."*

As Lucy grew older, her themes changed, mirroring the changes in her personality. Her tone became darker after the First World War and the horrific events she witnessed. Dr. Elizabeth Epperly, a Montgomery scholar, said: *"I don't think [the war] changed her outlook on nature, but I think it changed her outlook on human nature."*

Lucy suffered from severe depression. She tried to separate her work from her personal life, but her mental health took a toll on her and affected her writing. Even the themes in the Anne novels changed and became darker with time. Lucy grew with her characters, and they stopped being innocent with sunny personalities after the author saw the worst of humanity during the two world wars.

Lucy's Impact on Canadian Identity and the Literary World

Lucy is Canada's most famous and prominent author. She focused on Prince Edward Island's landscape and the Canadian culture as if they were characters in her novels. Most people who read *Anne of Green Gables* at the time didn't know that Prince Edward Island was a real place. They thought it was imaginary, like Wonderland, thanks to Lucy's enchanting narrative and portrayal of the island, which captured its peacefulness and beauty.

> *"You never know what peace is until you walk on the shores or in the fields or along the winding red roads of Prince Edward Island in a summer twilight when the dew is falling, and the old stars are peeping out, and the sea keeps its mighty tryst with the little land it loves."*

Lucy's books put Prince Edward Island on the map and influenced the tourism industry. Now, it attracts about 1.6 million tourists each year who want to walk in their favorite author and character's footsteps. The Green Gables House, which inspired Lucy's novel, has also become a famous landmark.

Lucy's literary works will survive the test of time. Her name is associated with great authors like Charles Dickens and Jane Austen. Her charming and loveable characters resonate with readers of all ages worldwide. Her novels are still popular and draw scholars' and critics' attention. In 2014, Anne Shirley was labeled "Canada's most iconic fictional character."

Anne of Green Gables was declared "Canada's most enduring literary export." BBC held a survey in 2003 ranking the best novels. *Anne of Green Gables* landed at number 40 ahead of Charles Dickens's *A Christmas Carol* and F. Scott Fitzgerald's *The Great Gatsby.*

The Handmaid's Tale, by Canadian author Margaret Atwood, described Anne as a feminist hero.

Her novels have been adapted into movies, TV shows, and plays, which helped introduce her work to new generations.

Global Reception

Lucy's fame was unprecedented for a Canadian author. In 1927, British Prime Minister Stanley Baldwin sent her a fan letter expressing her admiration for her work. She also met Prince Edward VIII of Wales before he became king. In 1925, *Anne of Green Gables* was translated into French, Finnish, Norwegian, Polish, Dutch, and Swedish. It was the fourth most popular book in Poland and was published in seven editions. It has also become a part of the Japanese school curriculum since 1952.

Many organizations and institutions worldwide are named *Green Gables* and Anne Shirley, such as the *Green Gables* beach houses in multiple countries and the *Green Gables* nursing school in Japan.

Lucy died in Toronto in 1942 and was buried in her favorite place, Prince Edward Island.

Facts About the Edwardian Era's Literary Scene

- The Edwardian era was a period in the 20th century between 1901 and 1914 and named after King Edward VII.
- Since it was a short era, Edwardian and Victorian writers such as Joseph Conrad and Arthur Conan Doyle overlap and are associated with both periods.
- E.M. Forster and George Bernard Shaw are considered the voices of the Edwardian era.
- Authors and poets in this era shifted from traditional storytelling to experimental storytelling, which used a character's stream of consciousness to capture their thought process.
- Most famous Edwardian-era literary works include E.M. Forster's *A Room With a View* (1908), George Bernard Shaw's *Pygmalion* (1912), and G.K. Chesterton's *The Man Who Was Thursday* (1908).
- The Edwardian era's main characteristics include questioning society, introducing popular, light, and fast-paced novels, criticizing imperialism, and discussing political and social issues such as colonialism, class system, and women's suffrage.

Lucy had a hard life but tried to conceal it from society and the world. However, her pain was often reflected in her characters' struggles and dark themes, especially in her later novels. Some modern-day scholars believe that if one examines Lucy's themes, one will find that they have always been dark but hidden behind some of her charming characters and beautiful imagery.

Lucy should be remembered as the author of *Anne of Green Gables* and also as a literary icon who created different characters that touch people's hearts and universal themes that will remain relevant for centuries.

Chapter 9: Wilfrid Laurier and the Dawn of the 20th Century

In the history of any country, certain figures emerge not only as leaders but as architects of national identity. Among these luminaries stands Wilfrid Laurier, a statesman whose legacy is more than just political. As Canada's seventh Prime Minister, Laurier's tenure from 1896 to 1911 witnessed the nation's transformation from a fledgling dominion to a confident player on the global stage. His profound influence on Canadian politics, culture, and identity still has a big impact today. This chapter will tell the tale of Wilfred Laurier and why he remains a towering figure in Canadian history.

Minister Wilfrid Laurier.
https://commons.wikimedia.org/wiki/File:Sir_Wilfrid_Laurier_M.P._April_1874.jpg

Early Life

Wilfrid Laurier came from a long line of Canadians who spoke French and followed the Roman Catholic faith. His family's story stretched back to the early days of New France, where ancestors like Augustin Hébert and Francois Cottineau-Champlaurier played important roles in building and defending the colony.

In 1815, Wilfrid's father, Carolus, was born. He dropped the name Cottineau and was baptized simply as Laurier. Carolus married Marcelle Martineau, and they built a home in the village of Saint-Lin. A devoted reader, Marcelle likely named their son Wilfrid after a character in a novel she admired. Unfortunately, Marcelle passed away from tuberculosis when Wilfrid was just seven years old.

After Marcelle's death, Carolus struggled to care for Wilfrid and his sickly sister, Malvina. He eventually proposed to Adeline Ethier, who had helped care for Marcelle in her final days. Adeline became a loving stepmother to Wilfrid and Malvina, and they cherished her deeply.

Wilfrid looked up to his father, Carolus, who was well-liked in their community and served as mayor of Saint-Lin for several years. Carolus was intelligent and outspoken, often challenging the Church's involvement in politics. He had a knack for friendly debates, a trait that Wilfrid inherited.

Watching his father settle disputes as a land surveyor, Wilfrid learned the value of compromise and seeing issues from multiple perspectives. These experiences shaped Wilfrid's beliefs and approach to problem-solving throughout his life.

Carolus believed strongly in education, knowing it was key to Wilfrid's success in life. Seeing that there were no boys' schools in Saint-Lin, Carolus and Marcelle taught Wilfrid at home until he was ten. Then, Carolus decided it was time for Wilfrid to learn more than just the basics, but he didn't want Wilfrid to learn in French or stay in their village. Back then, all the important businesses were run by English speakers, so Carolus wanted Wilfrid to be bilingual.

They sent Wilfrid to New Glasgow, a village twelve kilometers away, where most people spoke English. There, he attended Fort Rose School, which was open to everyone, regardless of religion. The only teacher, Sandy Maclean, taught all subjects. Wilfrid stayed with the Kirkes, an Irish Catholic family, and worked at John Murray's tailor shop, a Scottish Protestant. It was tough for Wilfrid to be away from home at such a young age, but he managed to stay positive, knowing it was what his father wanted.

In New Glasgow, Wilfrid quickly learned English with help from Sandy Maclean and John Murray. He fell in love with English literature and the beauty of the language. Even though he was Catholic, he attended Protestant religious classes and listened eagerly when John Murray read the Bible aloud. This love for English stayed with Wilfrid throughout his life.

Collège de L'Assomption

In September 1854, at thirteen, Wilfrid Laurier began his journey into adolescence by enrolling at the Collège de L'Assomption, a Roman Catholic school located in the village of L'Assomption. It was quite different from his previous school experiences. However, Wilfrid faced a physical challenge – a condition that left him unable to engage in physically demanding activities without triggering violent coughing fits. This challenge reached a new level of seriousness when he experienced a frightening episode during a walk with a friend, resulting in coughing up blood.

Academically, Wilfrid excelled, particularly in languages and debate. He developed a deep love for words in French, English, and Latin, spending hours immersed in literature. His passion for debate flourished at L'Assomption, where he honed his skills in argumentation and public speaking. Inspired by local lawyers, especially Joseph Papineau, Wilfrid became fascinated with law and politics, setting his sights on a career in law. Despite occasional clashes with school authorities over his tardiness due to court visits, Wilfrid remained undeterred in his pursuit of knowledge and his dream of becoming a lawyer.

In the spring of 1861, just shy of his twentieth birthday, Wilfrid Laurier graduated from L'Assomption, ready to embark on the next phase of his journey into adulthood. Despite lingering doubts about his health, he felt a growing confidence in his abilities, poised to make his mark on the world.

Legal Education

In 1861, Wilfrid Laurier started his legal education journey at McGill University in Montreal, driven by a determination to succeed in both French and English law. Balancing his studies with practical experience, Laurier worked in the law office of Rodolphe Laflamme while attending lectures at McGill. Evenings were dedicated to studying, legal work, and indulging his love for literature, especially the works of Shakespeare, Burns, and Milton. His passion for debate flourished, and he became one of the university's most respected debaters.

Laurier's involvement in politics grew during his time at McGill, influenced by Laflamme's connections to the Rouge (or Liberal party). He shared the Rouge's belief in progress through change and championed freedom of thought and speech. Despite opposition from the Roman Catholic Church, which held significant political sway, Laurier remained committed to his political convictions.

At his graduation from McGill in May 1864, Laurier delivered a speech that reflected his deep-seated beliefs in justice, patriotism, and unity among Canada's diverse population. He emphasized the importance of embracing differences and working toward a harmonious society. It was during this speech that Laurier made a personal pledge to dedicate his life to fostering reconciliation and harmony among Canada's various communities.

Early Career

Wilfrid Laurier's immediate priority after graduating was establishing himself as a lawyer and securing a livelihood. However, his early career was fraught with challenges. Two partnerships in the first two years post-graduation proved unsuccessful, leaving Laurier overworked, physically weakened, and struggling with his health. In October 1866, he suffered a severe health setback, collapsing in his office after coughing up blood.

During this difficult time, Antoine-Aimé Dorion, a Rouge party leader, approached Laurier with a proposition. Dorion suggested that Laurier take over Le Défricheur, a small newspaper in L'Avenir, while also practicing law in the countryside. Laurier, seeing an opportunity for a slower pace of life and hoping for an improvement in his health, accepted the offer and moved to L'Avenir in November 1866.

Antoine-Aimé Dorion.
https://commons.wikimedia.org/wiki/File:AntoineAimeDorion23.jpg

However, Laurier's hopes were dashed as he struggled to garner interest in both his legal services and the newspaper. His health did not improve, and after a month, he relocated to Victoriaville, unaware that he was walking into a trap set by the ultramontane Monseigneur Laflèche. In Victoriaville, Laurier faced relentless attacks from local priests who denounced him as a threat to the Church and its teachings.

Despite his efforts to defend himself and the Rouge's beliefs in Le Défricheur, the newspaper suffered a decline in sales, and Laurier fell into debt. His law practice also floundered, exacerbating his financial and health woes. Faced with mounting pressure and unable to cope with the opposition, Laurier declared bankruptcy and ceased publication of Le Défricheur, marking the end of his first major confrontation with the Church.

Laurier's defeat taught him a valuable lesson: he needed to prioritize stabilizing his financial situation before engaging in political campaigns. Determined to succeed as a lawyer, he sought Arthabaska, a picturesque town with a thriving legal scene. In September 1867, he moved to Arthabaska, where he established his fifth law practice, hoping for a fresh start and a path toward success.

Love and Relationship

Wilfrid Laurier's life took a significant turn during his time in Montreal. While renting a room from Dr. Séraphin Gauthier and his wife Phoebé, he met Zoë, the daughter of another boarder. Zoë, a talented pianist, captured Laurier's heart with her hazel eyes and musical skill. Their relationship blossomed, and they fell deeply in love, enjoying each other's company and sharing moments of happiness.

However, as their love grew, Zoë expressed her desire for marriage, longing for a deeper commitment from Laurier. She pleaded with him to consider their future together despite his concerns about his health, financial stability, and uncertain career prospects as a lawyer. Consumed by his worries and ambitions, Laurier remained hesitant to commit to marriage, fearing that he couldn't provide a stable life for Zoë.

Despite their love for each other, Laurier's stubbornness and fear of failure cooled their relationship. When Pierre Valois, a medical student, expressed his intentions to marry Zoë, she eventually agreed, feeling that Laurier's silence on the matter indicated a lack of commitment.

However, fate intervened when Dr. Gauthier summoned Laurier to Montreal urgently. Dr. Gauthier's examination revealed that Laurier did not have tuberculosis as he had feared but rather chronic bronchitis, a condition manageable with treatment. Moreover, Dr. Gauthier revealed Zoë's true feelings, explaining that she was hopelessly in love with Laurier and deeply distressed about her impending marriage to Valois.

With renewed hope and clarity, Laurier realized that he couldn't let Zoë slip away. Despite the uncertainties, he decided to take a chance on love. Rushing to Zoë's side, he declared his love and proposed marriage. Overwhelmed with emotion, Zoë accepted, and they decided to marry that very day.

Political Achievements

The Conservative victory marked a temporary setback for Laurier. Despite losing his cabinet position, he managed to retain his seat in Quebec East, which was crucial for his legal career. Over the next four years, his growing public profile attracted clients to his law office, resulting in a thriving practice with his partner, Joseph Lavergne.

As Laurier settled into his role alongside Liberal leader Edward Blake in Parliament, the tranquility of his political career was disrupted by news of a rebellion in the North-West Territories led by Louis Riel, a figure with a controversial past. Riel's history as a Métis leader and his involvement in previous uprisings had left a deep divide in Canadian society.

The rebellion ignited tensions between English and French Canadians, as opinions on Riel's actions varied widely across the country. While many in Quebec viewed him as a defender of French-speaking Catholics, others saw him as a criminal and a threat to stability. Riel's eventual capture and subsequent trial sparked outrage in Quebec, leading to mass protests and the emergence of the Parti National, a political entity championing the rights of French-speaking Catholics.

When Parliament reconvened three months later, Laurier had ample time to reflect on recent events. He keenly grasped the gravity of the Métis uprising and Louis Riel's execution. The longstanding division between English and French Canadians had not only resurfaced but now posed a threat to national unity. It was a critical moment for Laurier to uphold his longstanding commitment to fostering harmony between francophones and anglophones.

As Laurier assumed the leadership of the Liberal Party in 1887, he faced a nation grappling with internal divisions. Francophone-anglophone tensions were escalating, exacerbated by the fallout from Louis Riel's execution. The emergence of the Parti National in Quebec reflected the anger of many francophones toward the federal government's perceived favoritism toward anglophone Protestants.

On the other hand, anglophone Canadians, largely of English descent, maintained strong ties to Britain, viewing their loyalty to the empire as paramount. Imperialists like D'Alton McCarthy, a Conservative MP, advocated for a singular British identity, often at the expense of minority groups, particularly francophone Roman Catholics.

Laurier, drawing on his vision of Canadian nationalism, sought a path of tolerance and inclusivity. He believed that true unity could only be achieved by respecting and preserving the cultural identities of all Canadians. Recognizing the importance of provincial autonomy, Laurier advocated for each province's right to govern its affairs without federal interference, thereby safeguarding minority rights.

However, this vision faced significant challenges, particularly during the Manitoba Schools Crisis. The Manitoba government's decision to abolish French as an official language and restrict Catholic education sparked outrage among Roman Catholics. The federal government's reluctance to intervene highlighted the delicate balance between provincial autonomy and minority rights.

First French-Speaking Prime Minister

The subsequent general election in June 1896 delivered a resounding victory for Laurier and the Liberals. Despite opposition from the Roman Catholic Church, Laurier's promise of a just and inclusive approach resonated with Quebec voters. With a strong majority in the House of Commons, Laurier became Canada's first French-speaking, Roman Catholic prime minister, heralding a new era of leadership guided by principles of tolerance, unity, and respect for diversity.

The opening of Parliament in August 1896 marked a significant moment for Laurier and the Liberals, who celebrated their return to power after eighteen years in opposition. With a talented cabinet comprising individuals like Mowat, Fielding, and Blair, Laurier set out to address pressing issues, notably the Manitoba schools crisis.

Despite the backlash from some quarters, Laurier remained steadfast in his belief that the compromise was essential for maintaining national unity and protecting minority rights. When the Quebec clergy persisted in their opposition, Laurier sought intervention from Pope Leo XIII, who issued a directive urging acceptance of the compromise.

Laurier's diplomatic success extended beyond Canada's borders, as evidenced by his reception during the Diamond Jubilee celebrations in London. Knighted by Queen Victoria and celebrated as a prominent figure in the empire, Laurier capitalized on the opportunity to strengthen ties with Britain while emphasizing Canada's growing sense of national identity.

However, Laurier's approach to imperial relations was nuanced. While he expressed admiration for Britain and emphasized Canada's British heritage, he also asserted Canada's status as a nation and resisted British attempts to exert control over colonial affairs. His refusal to commit Canadian troops to British wars and his cautious approach to the proposed imperial council at the Colonial Conference reflected his commitment to preserving Canadian autonomy.

In the aftermath of the conference, Laurier received further recognition in France, where he was honored with the Legion of Honour. His triumphant return to Canada was marked by widespread acclaim, signaling Canada's emergence as a respected player on the world stage.

Tenure as PM

Laurier's tenure as Prime Minister was marked by both triumphs and challenges. His approach to the Manitoba schools' question demonstrated his willingness to compromise for the sake of national unity, earning praise from many Canadians. However, his stance on Canada's involvement in the Boer War created controversy and division within the country.

When tensions arose in South Africa, Laurier faced the difficult task of balancing Canadian sentiment with Britain's expectations. While many Canadians supported the idea of assisting the mother country, others, particularly in Quebec, vehemently opposed involvement. Laurier's decision to allow volunteers to join the British forces while avoiding official Canadian troop deployment was a compromise aimed at appeasing both sides.

Despite facing criticism, Laurier maintained his commitment to national unity and pursued policies aimed at fostering economic growth and development, such as encouraging immigration to the West and promoting railway expansion. However, his decision to involve the government in railway construction proved controversial and ultimately led to the proliferation of competing railway lines, highlighting the challenges of balancing economic development with responsible governance.

Throughout his tenure, Laurier remained optimistic about Canada's future and steadfast in his belief in the country's potential on the world stage. However, challenges such as the unresolved boundary dispute with the United States served as reminders of the complexities of Canadian nationhood and the need for prudent leadership in navigating domestic and international affairs.

Cracks began to appear within the government, signaling the onset of the decay that often accompanies prolonged political dominance. Allegations of corruption swirled around some of Laurier's cabinet ministers, particularly Clifford Sifton, the minister of the interior, who was accused of exploiting his position for personal gain. Two other ministers were forced to resign – one for corrupt election practices and the other for alcohol abuse – further tarnishing Laurier's cabinet.

Yet, the most significant threat to Laurier's leadership came from Henri Bourassa, a former ally turned adversary. Despite recognizing Bourassa's talents and initially entrusting him with parliamentary responsibilities, irreconcilable differences emerged between them. Bourassa, a staunch Catholic and ultramontane, vehemently opposed Laurier's policies, particularly regarding the role of religion in politics and Canada's relationship with Great Britain.

Henri Bourassa.

Bourassa's influence grew, especially among young francophones who rallied behind his vision of "la survivance" and nationalism, which eventually fostered separatist sentiments in Quebec. The creation of Saskatchewan and Alberta as provinces further fueled tensions between Laurier and Bourassa, particularly regarding the contentious issue of separate school systems.

A single word shattered Laurier's dreams of retirement: dreadnought. In 1909, as Germany began constructing super battleships dubbed dreadnoughts, Britain saw this as a direct challenge to its naval dominance. The call for more British dreadnoughts reignited the debate in Canada over its role in supporting the mother country militarily. While Quebec and rural areas opposed involvement, most Canadians favored aiding Britain. Reflecting this sentiment, the Conservative Opposition demanded Canada take responsibility for protecting its coastline and contribute money for dreadnought construction if the danger to Britain escalated.

Losses and Defeats

As the reciprocity debate intensified, Laurier found himself attacked from all sides, labeled a traitor in Quebec and Ontario alike. Despite his efforts to campaign vigorously, Laurier faced hostility, even violence, in his own province. The election results, with significant losses in Ontario and Quebec, sealed Laurier's political fate. Two weeks after the devastating defeat, he resigned as prime minister, his once bright political career now eclipsed by the first taste of defeat.

Despite his bitter defeat, Laurier made an astonishingly rapid recovery. He thrived on competition, and although it caused him pain, it also served as his remedy. *"I am young in everything but the arithmetic of years,"* he soon quipped to an audience. *"I don't feel ripe for heaven, and in any case, I want another tussle with the Tories."* Eager to rejoin the political fray, he found himself in the House of Commons five days before his seventieth birthday for the opening of the new session of Parliament in November 1911. After fifteen years, he was once again the leader of the Opposition.

The conclusion of the bitter campaign, just days before Christmas, cast a shadow over the holiday season for the Lauriers. Despite the electoral setback, they gathered with family and friends, finding solace in each other's company. Laurier allowed himself only a brief respite before resuming his political endeavors. Recognizing the isolation both he and Quebec faced, he resolved to continue the fight, understanding that abandoning his province, country, and party was not an option. His duty remained clear: to keep Quebec within Canada despite the deep divisions caused by conscription.

However, Laurier's health began to falter, culminating in a stroke that would ultimately claim his life. On February 22, 1919, thousands gathered to bid farewell to the esteemed statesman as his funeral procession wound through the streets of Ottawa. His passing marked the end of an era, leaving behind a legacy of leadership, integrity, and unwavering dedication to Canada.

Zoë survived Laurier for a short time before joining him in eternal rest, fulfilling her wish to be buried beside her beloved husband. Together, they lie in Notre Dame Cemetery, their shared tomb bearing the simple yet profound inscription: Laurier. Indeed, that name is enough to capture the legacy of one of Canada's greatest statesmen.

Chapter 10: Wayne Gretzky and the Evolution of Hockey in Canada

Wayne Gretzky is what you get when you add natural ability to a ridiculous work ethic. Many athletes have been the best in their era, but a flood of Gretzky records still holds this legend as the greatest of all time. Wayne Gretzky revolutionized hockey, reaching new audiences and growing the sport beyond niche communities. His conduct off the ice sets him apart as a role model for upcoming athletes.

Wayne Gretzky revolutionized hockey.
The original uploader was Hakandahlstrom at English Wikipedia. Later versions were uploaded by IrisKawling at en.wikipedia., CC BY-SA 3.0 <https://creativecommons.org/licenses/by-sa/3.0>, via Wikimedia Commons. https://commons.wikimedia.org/wiki/File:Wgretz.jpg

Gretzkey's dominance has not yet been replicated. He perfected all parts of his game and seemed to have no flaws. Gretzkey's longevity performing at levels no one could match displayed his dedication to the game. However, his impact was not limited to the sport. Gretzky's philanthropic efforts have helped uplift young players, and his charity work has served the unfortunate from many backgrounds.

Gretzky evolved from an electrifying player to working behind the scenes to continue to carry the sport forward. His commitment on the ice has now been transformed into business excellence as an entrepreneur. Even though he has shifted gears into a business role, he still loves the game and keeps an eye out for new talent. Wayne Gretzky is the symbol of sporting excellence and can be placed on an athlete Mount Rushmore alongside all of the greats.

Gretzky embodies the spirit of a true sportsman. His focus propelled him to the top of hockey and transformed the sport, taking his teammates and opponents to heights they couldn't have imagined. Gretzky understood that although he had individual skills, hockey was a team sport. Therefore, he always pushed those around him to keep up with his elite level. As a leader, player, and role model, Gretzky is Canada's biggest sporting export.

A Hockey Prodigy

Wayne Gretzky was born with a pair of skates on his feet in Ontario in 1961. His father, Walter, built an ice rink in their backyard, which would change young Wayne's life. Gretzky learned to skate before he could walk and spent hours in the backyard to improve his passing, shooting, and gliding skills. By the tender age of only two years old, Gretzky had begun skating. He immediately fell in love with it, and his parents encouraged their son's enjoyment of hockey and skating. Once they put a hockey stick in his hand, everything changed. From that moment, Gretzky understood what he wanted to dedicate his life to.

Gretzky's skill was beyond his age, so his father signed him up in the 10-year-old division when he was only six. In his first season, he did not cope well with the bigger children who overpowered him. Gretzky realized that he was going to have to out-skill the bigger players so their size did not influence the outcomes. He grew one goal from the first season to 378 in the last.

As a teenager, Gretzky played in the Ontario Hockey Association's league. He was only there for one season but finished as the second-highest scorer. He then competed in the 1978 World Junior Championships, but this time, he was the top scorer. The budding superstar's talent was hard to miss. Gretzky's professional debut was for the Indianapolis Racers, where he placed 25 games before the team folded. His contract was sold to the Edmonton Oilers, where he would achieve many of his career's most legendary feats.

Some would argue that Wayne Gretzky never became "The Great One" but always was one of a kind. At age 6, Gretzky spent eight hours a day on the ice, driven by pure love. His singular obsession propelled him to the heights of the sport that no one has reached since. Although the game has grown since Gretzky's era, his dominance still has not been replicated.

He was one of a few rookies to win the Most Valuable Player award and was considered among the best before he turned pro. His school career and early NHL performances showed that he was something special. Gretzky managed to keep up his inspiring performances, showing that he was not a flash in the pan. His staying power and ability to perform left onlookers amazed constantly. His sporting story still stuns anybody who gets introduced to it for the first time, continually elevating the Great One to mythic status.

Gretzky struggled with an intense fear of failure from his childhood. His love for the game caused him a lot of anxiety because his desire to be the best burned so deeply. Gretzky mentions how his fear evolved during his career. When he was 9, he feared he wouldn't make the team. The terror of losing spilled over into his NHL career. When Gretzky experienced a period of draught remaining goalless, the anxiety from his childhood grew within him. Gretzky explains how he used his fear to give him an edge because it motivated his hard work and gave him respect for his peers.

The Greatest of All Time

In terms of dominance, you think of Michael Jordan for basketball, Babe Ruth for baseball, and Wayne Gretzky for hockey. The gap between Gretzky and his peers made the game feel unfair. Reading hockey records books is just like repeatedly chanting Gretzky's name. He retired in 1999, yet many of the bars he set are still standing. After he retired, Gretzky was immediately inducted into the Hall of Fame. He holds the records for most career goals at 894, most assists in 1963, and most career points at 2867.

The 80s and 90s were a rough era for hockey. When modern viewers watch the games from this timeframe, they are shocked and wonder what the rules were! Bench brawls were excessively common, and players would injure one another far more than they do today. Gretzky was not the most physical player, but he was smooth. His swift movements made him so slippery that the bullying tactics that were common at that time did not work. Gretzky helped transition hockey to include more skill and teamwork because the brutish tactics of the past were no longer effective.

Gretzky cut through the ice like a demon on skates. His unmatched athleticism kept him moving at full speed throughout the game. Players struggled to keep up with him because he seemed to be more machine than man. His opponents' competitiveness could not fuel any hatred for Gretzky because although he dragged them along the ice, he always exhibited great sportsmanship by staying humble, looking to consistently improve, and honoring players.

Gretzky's playing style was unbeatable. He led the Oilers to Stanley Cup glory in 1984, 1985, 1987, and 1988. He came out the gate on fire, scoring 51 goals and making 86 assists in his first season. This won him the Hart Memorial Trophy for being the most valuable player in the league. He would go on to win the trophy another nine times. He would also finish as the league's top scorer for seven consecutive years.

The Stanley Cup.

Wayne Gretzky became the best player in NHL history because he balanced individual greatness with teamwork. Ken Dryden remarks, *"He was, I think, the first Canadian forward to play a true team game."* Gretzky understood that to create a winning team, they could not rely on the dominance of one man. So, he would craft plays as much as he scored. Gretzky was the hardest worker on the ice and expected all his teammates to keep up with his lightning movements. Gretzky persistently practiced every aspect of the sport.

His rapid rise and unprecedented dominance earned him the fan nickname "The Great One." Wayne Gretzky's obsession grew to unimaginable proportions in Canada. He had a mass-produced doll, and the Canadian government minted a one-dollar Wayne Gretzky coin. The Gretzky mania reached a fever pitch. Not only did the masses love him for his skills, but they also admired his soft-spoken nature.

Gretzky's playing style was fast-paced and intense. He moved the puck around quickly and would explode from set pieces. When he played, it was like he was hovering above the arena, seeing everyone from a bird's eye view. His game intelligence allowed him to predict movements and see openings like he had psychic visions. Gretzky explained that he never skated to where the puck was but went to where it would be. His ability to predict the game helped him set up amazing plays, which led to his having a record number of assists.

Gretzky brought the best out of his peers, but they pushed him to elevate his game as well. One of his biggest rivalries was against the Pittsburg Penguins' Mario Lemieux. When the Edmonton Oilers and Pittsburg Penguins met, the tension between the teams caused the ice to melt. Lemieux broke Gretzky's eight-year streak winning the Hart trophy. They played on the national team together, winning the Canada Cup. Gretzky passed the puck to Lemieux, giving him the chance to score the game-winning goal.

Gretzky was known for his precision and athleticism, but Lemieux was a maestro with stick control, wowing fans with his unique moves. Lemieux does not appear in the record books as often as Gretzky, but he's a legendary player in his own right. He spoke about Gretzky's humility, stating that he won the Hart trophy because Gretzky got injured and that playing alongside him on Team Canada helped inspire him. You'll never hear any of Gretzky's contemporaries saying a bad word about him, regardless of how intense their rivalries got. Gretzky was a beast on the ice, but he always remained an approachable gentleman with a heart of gold.

When Wayne Gretzky left the Edmonton Oilers for the Los Angeles Kings, he never managed to maintain the dominance he once had. This may have been because he did not have the same supporting players who helped elevate his greatness. However, he remained in the conversation for the shortlist of the best in the game. The closest he got to winning a Stanley Cup was in the final against the Montreal Canadiens, but unfortunately, they lost.

Gretzky then got transferred to the St. Louis Blues, where he played for only one season before getting traded to the New York Rangers, ending his incredible NHL career. He continued being active in the sport as an owner and coach. Furthermore, he supported young players, demonstrating the many benefits of competing in hockey.

Changing the Game

The dominance of the Oiler's forwards led to the NHL changing the rules to minimize the number of goals being scored. They are attempting to reverse many of these rules today because the shortsighted rule changes overlooked how special Gretzky was. They did not realize that other players would not match his dominance for decades. The game became more fast-paced, and the increase in popularity Gretzky facilitated helped get more invested in the sport.

Gretzky's career was not free from controversy. One of the games that hurt Gretzky's reputation, gaining him the title of cheater, was game six of the 1993 Western Conference final. The Los Angeles Kings were facing the Toronto Maple Leafs. In a game-changing moment, Gretzky committed a high-stick foul against Doug Gilmour. The referee, Kerry Fraser, did not make the call, which would have resulted in a penalty for Gretzky. The media ripped Gretzky apart, but the brunt of the heat fell on Kerry Fraser. The referee admits that the one regret he had in his career was making that bad call, stating that it would be the thing he'd change if he could go back in time.

Gilmour did not have anything negative to say about Gretzky, understanding that in the rough era of the 90s, things got heated in games. He is also more merciful to Fraser than he was to himself. He stated that the referee is only human and that everyone makes mistakes. However, Gilmour confided that when he rewatches the match, he gets frustrated with Fraser because he feels that the high stick is not the only bad call made in the game.

Gretzky's peers do not deny his greatness because the records speak for themselves, and he radiates positivity. The legend's athleticism increased the pace of hockey, and the precision he played with kept everyone on their toes. Gretzky also revealed the importance of being adaptable and adjusting your strategy during the game. Pundits would often comment on how Gretzky played – as if he had eyes in the back of his head.

Bringing Hockey to the Masses

People who haven't watched a single minute of a Hockey match know who Wayne Gretzky is. His cultural influence extended beyond the sport. When he was traded to the Los Angeles Kings, hockey's popularity went nuclear, expanding into unexpected markets. Wayne Gretzky was arguably the first real hockey superstar. As soon as he joined the Kings, the sport got a supercharged nitrous boost. Home game attendance for the Los Angeles Kings went up 30%.

California has a warm climate all year round, so there was never a demand for hockey in the state. However, when Gretzky made the state his home, people from around America started tuning in, and children all around the country wanted to join a team. Gretzky's superstardom as the greatest player to hold a hockey stick spread the popularity of the sport to regions like Texas and other temperate parts of the U.S. that had a huge football or basketball culture but never embraced hockey. This caused a hurricane of new players to emerge, hoping to rise to the dominance of Gretzky.

Doug Gilmour.

His impact on growing the sport was unfathomable. In California, a region where hockey never made an impact, high school leagues readily grew from four teams to 100 teams in the space of two years. The NHL started including more teams as investors saw a chance to ride this wave of popularity. It grew from 21 teams to the 32 teams that participate in the league today.

Gretzky was the ultimate celebrity in a city where stars were worshipped. Visits to his home by tourists were out of control. Tour buses would regularly stop near his home, hoping to get a glimpse of the legend. He gained so much fame that there was a repeat of the Gretzky fever that had gripped Canada during his time at the Edmonton Oilers. The brilliant player even hosted the popular sketch comedy show Saturday Night Live. He still holds a significant social media presence and regularly gets interviewed on numerous platforms.

Although his work on the ice will forever be admired, his biggest contribution to hockey was the new audiences he got the sport in front of. He never won a Stanley Cup with the Los Angeles Kings, but putting on that jersey may have led to the biggest achievement of his career, which was solidifying hockey as a sport to be reckoned with.

The Next Generation

As a child prodigy, Wayne Gretzky understood the importance of getting an early start. Gretzky's parents had him on the ice by two years old, which likely contributed to his natural understanding of the game. Not everyone has the opportunities he had, so to fill the gap and find talent in less fortunate communities, the icon set up the Wayne Gretzky Foundation. The non-profit organization is dedicated to developing young talent and funding players who cannot afford to play. This work in underprivileged communities aims to help keep children out of the negative influences of drugs and crime. Gretzky understands the power of sports, so he uses it as a tool of upliftment.

His philanthropic drive was active throughout his career and continued to thrive afterward. Gretzky raised awareness and donated to many causes, including charities that worked with blind people. He showed that athletes had the responsibility to be exemplary people because the masses' eyes were on them.

Wayne Gretzky's winning never stopped once he retired from the NHL. As the Executive Director of the national Canadian team, he won Olympic gold at the Salt Lake Games in 2002. This was after Canada had gone 50 years without claiming the top spot. Just like he revitalized hockey, he restored the Canadian team to its past glory. Since retiring, Gretzky has continued to be a presence in hockey, which has garnered many eyes. He has given his opinion on various matters in and outside of the sport and has been active in the political arena.

Gretzky bought a minority stake in the Phoenix Coyotes and later became the head coach. After an unremarkable stint with the team, Gretzky ran into financial troubles as the brand was losing money. His relationship with the NHL soured due to the money he owed from his time at the Phoenix Coyotes, but these issues eventually got resolved, and they managed to move past them. The Great One has had many business ventures and continues to enjoy financial success. He is a family man who stays out of negative media attention.

Gretzky's legacy is one of dedication and an insane work ethic. His love of the sport has propelled him to work with upcoming talent. Gretzky continues to follow the game closely, commenting on new players who may rise to his legacy. As the holder of 61 NHL records, he is still admired as the superstar every new player wants to be. Gretzky's captivating career and impeccable character uplift him as one of the greatest athletes of all time and a Canadian gem representing the country with class.

Generations that never got to see Gretzky play still shout his name to mimic his greatness when they push around a tennis ball on roller skates down a suburban road. The influence he had to propel hockey to new heights is still felt in the leagues and teams that sprung up in a post-Gretzky world. His career defined the sport for many people. Not only will Wayne Gretzky be remembered as The Great One, but his name will forever be tied to breathing life into the sport he loved.

Conclusion

Canadian history is a dazzling blend of all the individuals who contributed to its greatness. It all started when Sir John A. Macdonald, a lawyer born in Scotland and brought up in Upper Canada, merged the five provinces north of the United States into a single Dominion of Canada. He also became its first prime minister with a long and successful 19-year tenure.

That is how Canada was born, but it eventually became the second-largest country in the world due to the exploration efforts of John Franklin and his Inuit guides. Braving the risks of frostbite, hypothermia, ice storms, and the dangerous wildlife in the cold, he mapped large regions north of the Arctic Circle and discovered many new lands.

Fighting against the elements eventually gave way to battling against other nations to gain and preserve Canada's independence. Sir Arthur Currie and Agnes Macphail, with their staunch military leadership and smart political advocacy, were central in shaping history.

Long before the two World Wars, another fierce battle fought in Quebec brought the Canadian provinces under British rule, thanks to the military hero James Wolfe. The battle ended in 1759, with the British taking control of Quebec from the French.

World Wars and battles for supremacy aside, Viola Desmond and Nellie McClung fought the good fight – a crusade against social inequality. Their activism efforts not only led to equal voting rights for women but also paved the way for racial equality in the country. McClung was also an author, but she was focused on bringing social change.

The world-renowned Lucy Maud Montgomery brought about literary change. Her children's fiction novels are still narrated as bedtime stories. Another influential figure, Alexander Graham Bell, brought communication to its pinnacle with the groundbreaking invention of the telephone. This simple device would go on to advance many industries and fields of study around the world.

Technological progress didn't negatively affect environmental conservation, mostly thanks to Grey Owl (Archibald Belaney), who adopted the Indigenous culture and fought for the preservation of nature.

In modern Canada, two notable figures stand out. Wilfrid Laurier, one of the most influential prime ministers of all time, was known for his magnetic personality and keen political acumen. He was responsible for cementing Canada on the world map and introducing game-changing policies in the government. Second is Wayne Gretzky, who left a memorable impression on the ice hockey rink in the 1970s, '80s, and '90s with his mad skills.

Looking back on all these pivotal moments in Canada's history has inspired many more to help shape a better future. Although these notable historical figures transformed the country for the better, there is still potential for further change.

If you enjoyed this book, a review on Amazon would be greatly appreciated because it would mean a lot to hear from you.

To leave a review:
1. Open your camera app.
2. Point your mobile device at the QR code.
3. The review page will appear in your web browser.

Thanks for your support!

Check out another book in the series

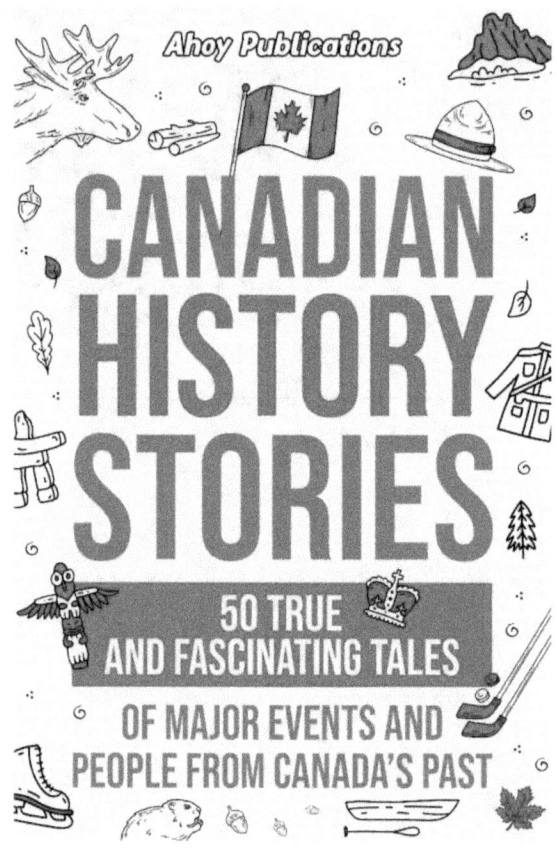

Welcome Aboard, Check Out This Limited-Time Free Bonus!

Ahoy, reader! Welcome to the Ahoy Publications family, and thanks for snagging a copy of this book! Since you've chosen to join us on this journey, we'd like to offer you something special.

Check out the link below for a FREE e-book filled with delightful facts about American History.

But that's not all - you'll also have access to our exclusive email list with even more free e-books and insider knowledge. Well, what are ye waiting for? Click the link below to join and set sail toward exciting adventures in American History.

Access your bonus here
https://ahoypublications.com/
Or, Scan the QR code!

References

Alex, T., er, & Foundation, M. B. L. (2021, October 1). Alexander Graham Bell Biography – Alexander & Mabel Bell. Www.belllegacy.org. https://www.belllegacy.org/articles/alexander-graham-bells-biography/

Alexander Graham Bell biography – Science Hall of Fame – National Library of Scotland. (n.d.). Digital.nls.uk. https://digital.nls.uk/scientists/biographies/alexander-graham-bell/index.html

Alexander Graham Bell: Inventor of the Telephone. (2018). Ducksters.com. https://www.ducksters.com/biography/alexander_graham_bell.php

Battle of Quebec. (n.d.). Www.nam.ac.uk. https://www.nam.ac.uk/explore/battle-quebec

Bayliss, R. (2002). Sir John Franklin's Last Arctic Expedition: A Medical Disaster. JRSM, 95(3), 151–153. https://doi.org/10.1258/jrsm.95.3.151

BBC – History – Alexander Graham Bell. (2014). Www.bbc.co.uk. https://www.bbc.co.uk/history/historic_figures/bell_alexander_graham.shtml

Bélanger, R. (2018). Sir Wilfrid Laurier | The Canadian Encyclopedia. Thecanadianencyclopedia.ca. https://www.thecanadianencyclopedia.ca/en/article/sir-wilfrid-laurier

Bingham, R. (2013, January 27). Viola Desmond | The Canadian Encyclopedia. The Canadian Encyclopedia. https://www.thecanadianencyclopedia.ca/en/article/viola-desmond

Biography. (2019, September 9). Alexander Graham Bell – Inventions, Telephone & Facts. Biography. https://www.biography.com/inventors/alexander-graham-bell

Black History Month: Remembering Canadian Civil Rights Icon Viola Desmond. (2016, February 7). CBC. https://www.cbc.ca/news/canada/viola-desmond-wanda-robson-black-history-month-1.3430629

Brower, K. (1990). Grey Owl – 90.01. Www.theatlantic.com. https://www.theatlantic.com/past/docs/issues/90jan/greyowl.htm

Canadian Leaders – Sir Wilfrid Laurier. (n.d.). Canada and the First World War. https://www.warmuseum.ca/firstworldwar/history/people/canadian-leaders/sir-wilfrid-laurier/

Cavanaugh, C., & McLeod, S. (2018). Irene Parlby | The Canadian Encyclopedia. Thecanadianencyclopedia.ca. https://www.thecanadianencyclopedia.ca/en/article/mary-irene-parlby

Chatterjee, S. (2022, December 28). "I Was Like That in School Too": Wayne Gretzky's Unhealthy Childhood Habit Once Carried Over to the NHL. EssentiallySports. https://www.essentiallysports.com/us-sports-news-nhl-news-i-was-like-that-in-school-too-wayne-gretzkys-unhealthy-childhood-habit-once-carried-over-to-the-nhl/

de Bruin, T. (2008, April 1). Agnes Macphail | The Canadian Encyclopedia. Thecanadianencyclopedia.ca. https://www.thecanadianencyclopedia.ca/en/article/agnes-macphail

Edwardian: Era, Characteristics & Literature. (n.d.). Vaia. https://www.vaia.com/en-us/explanations/english-literature/literary-movements/edwardian/

Eggington, R. (n.d.). James Wolfe. Historic UK. https://www.historic-uk.com/HistoryUK/HistoryofBritain/James-Wolfe/

Elite Prospects – Gretzky vs. Lemieux: A Timeless Debate of Hockey Greatness. (2023, October 11). Www.eliteprospects.com. https://www.eliteprospects.com/page/wayne-gretzky-vs-mario-lemieux-a-clash-of-hockey-legends

Fitzpatrick, K. (2006). Cultural Advice. Australian Dictionary of Biography; National Centre of Biography, Australian National University. https://adb.anu.edu.au/biography/franklin-sir-john-2066

Fox, L. (2016, June 7). Kerry Fraser Opens up about Gretzky's High Stick on Gilmour.Www.sportsnet.ca. https://www.sportsnet.ca/hockey/nhl/kerry-fraser-would-take-back-high-sticking-call-wayne-gretzky-doug-gilmour-game-6-1993-maple-leafs-kings/

George, C. (2021, May 6). 10 Favourite Quotes of Sir John A. Macdonald | By George Journal. Www.bygeorgejournal.ca. https://www.bygeorgejournal.ca/?p=2722

Government of Canada. (2017, August 11). About The Crown. Www.canada.ca. https://www.canada.ca/en/canadian-heritage/services/crown-canada/about.html#a1

Grey Highlands Public Library. (2018, November 13). Welcome to the Agnes Macphail Website. Www.greyhighlandspubliclibrary.com . https://www.greyhighlandspubliclibrary.com/AgnesMacphail/

H. Marsh, J. (n.d.). Sir Wilfrid Laurier: the Politics of Compromise | The Canadian Encyclopedia. Www.thecanadianencyclopedia.ca. https://www.thecanadianencyclopedia.ca/en/article/laurier-the-first-canadian-feature

Hallett, M. E. (2018, October 3). Nellie McClung | The Canadian Encyclopedia. Thecanadianencyclopedia.ca. https://www.thecanadianencyclopedia.ca/en/article/nellie-letitia-mcclung

Hastings Museum and Art Gallery. (n.d.). Grey Owl – Hastings Museum and Art Gallery. Hastings Museum and Art Gallery. https://www.hmag.org.uk/explore/stories/grey-owl/

Hasty, A. (2024, February 4). Lucy Maud Montgomery: A Literary Legacy of Endearing Characters and Timeless Stories. Hasty Book List. https://www.hastybooklist.com/blog/lucy-maud-montgomery

Historica Canada Teacher Community. (n.d.). Agnes Macphail | Historica Canada Education Portal. Education.historica canada.ca. http://education.historicacanada.ca/en/tools/106

History Spotlight: Sir Wilfrid Laurier – Canada's History. (2015). Canadashistory.ca. https://www.canadashistory.ca/explore/prime-ministers/history-spotlight-sir-wilfrid-laurier

History.com Editors. (2009, November 2). Battle of Quebec (1759). HISTORY. https://www.history.com/topics/native-american-history/battle-of-quebec-1759

Hyatt, A. m.j. (2017). Sir Arthur Currie | The Canadian Encyclopedia. Thecanadianencyclopedia.ca. https://www.thecanadianencyclopedia.ca/en/article/sir-arthur-currie

Jackel, S. (2008, April 1). Emily Murphy. The Canadian Encyclopedia. https://www.thecanadianencyclopedia.ca/en/article/emily-murphy

Jackson, C. M. (2022, May 5). Emily of New Moon Trilogy. LitReaderNotes. https://www.litreadernotes.com/home/2022/4/5/emily-of-new-moon-trilogy

James Wolfe: The Heroic Martyr. (2019). Nam.ac.uk. https://www.nam.ac.uk/explore/James-Wolfe

John A. Macdonald. (2021). Www.cbc.ca. https://www.cbc.ca/history/EPCONTENTSE1EP8CH3PA1LE.html

Johnson, J. K., & Waite, P. B. (1990). Biography – MacDonald, Sir John Alexander – Volume XII (1891-1900) – Dictionary of Canadian Biography. Www.biographi.ca. http://www.biographi.ca/en/bio/macdonald_john_alexander_12E.html

Kellie Elrick. (2024, March 12). Revisiting Lucy Maud Montgomery. The Tribune. https://www.thetribune.ca/a-e/revisiting-lucy-maud-montgomery-12032024/

Klavon, K. (2014, January 4). Why Wayne Gretzky is the Greatest Athlete Ever. Bleacher Report; Bleacher Report. https://bleacherreport.com/articles/1906423-why-wayne-gretzky-is-the-greatest-athlete-ever

Lemieux Breaks Gretzky's 8-Yaer String of MVP Awards. (1988, June 9). Deseret News. https://www.deseret.com/1988/6/9/18768354/lemieux-breaks-gretzky-s-8-year-string-of-mvp-awards/

Louis-Joseph de Montcalm. (n.d.). American Battlefield Trust. https://www.battlefields.org/learn/biographies/louis-joseph-de-montcalm

MacKay, P. (n.d.). John A. Macdonald, The Indispensable Politician. Macdonald-Laurier Institute. https://macdonaldlaurier.ca/confederation-project/john-a-macdonald/

Magazine, S., & Braganza, V. M. (2023, May). The Author of "Anne of Green Gables" Lived a Far Less Charmed Life Than Her Beloved Heroine. Smithsonian Magazine. https://www.smithsonianmag.com/arts-culture/lm-montgomery-anne-green-gables-life-180981839/

McGill University. (2023, April 3). Sir Arthur Currie, 1920-1933. Office of the President and Vice-Chancellor. https://www.mcgill.ca/president/article/past-principals/sir-arthur-currie-1920-1933

McIntosh, A., & Devereux, C. (2013, January 1). Lucy Maud Montgomery | The Canadian Encyclopedia. Thecanadianencyclopedia.ca. https://www.thecanadianencyclopedia.ca/en/article/montgomery-lucy-maud

McIntosh, A., Gagnon, C., & Besner, N. (2009, March 26). Anne of Green Gables | The Canadian Encyclopedia. Www.thecanadianencyclopedia.ca. https://www.thecanadianencyclopedia.ca/en/article/anne-of-green-gables

McLeod, S. (2016, February 11). Carrie Best | The Canadian Encyclopedia. Www.thecanadianencyclopedia.ca. https://www.thecanadianencyclopedia.ca/en/article/carrie-best

Milestones: 1750–1775 – Office of the Historian. (n.d.). History.state.gov. https://history.state.gov/milestones/1750-1775/french-indian-war

Nast, C. (2023, October 11). Wayne Gretzky, Hockey's GOAT, Is Still the Sport's Biggest Booster: "Everybody Has to Be an Ambassador." Vanity Fair. https://www.vanityfair.com/news/2023/10/wayne-gretzky-hockey-tnt

Nielsen, L. A. (2019, September 18). Grey Owl, Pioneering Conservationist in Canada, Born (1888). Today in Conservation. https://todayinconservation.com/2019/06/september-18-grey-owl-pioneering-conservationist-in-canada-born-1888/

O'Brien, S. (2017, October 5). 13 Things You Didn't Know about Sir John Franklin's Doomed Arctic Expedition | Boundless by CSMA. Www.boundless.co.uk. https://www.boundless.co.uk/news-competitions/lifestyle/13-things-about-sir-john-franklin-expedition

Pacheco, A. (n.d.). Anne of Green Gables: A Multi-Generational Experience. Www.anneofgreengables.com. https://www.anneofgreengables.com/blog-posts/anne-of-green-gables-a-multi-generational-experience

Parliament of Canada. (2019). Women's Right to Vote in Canada. Parl.ca. https://lop.parl.ca/sites/ParlInfo/default/en_CA/ElectionsRidings/womenVote

Petrovic, Jean. (2021). Celebrating Viola Desmond, Carrie Best, and a New Philatelic Acquisition.Blogs.bl.uk. https://blogs.bl.uk/americas/2021/12/viola-desmond-etc.html

Prahl, A. (n.d.). The Fascinating, Heartbreaking Life of "Anne of Green Gables" Author. ThoughtCo. https://www.thoughtco.com/lucy-maud-montgomery-author-4586962

Ramesar, V. (2022, February 8). Wanda Robson, Activist Who Championed Legacy of Her Sister Viola Desmond, Dies at 95.CBC. https://www.cbc.ca/news/canada/nova-scotia/wanda-robson-viola-desmond-death-1.6342349

ScienCentral, mailto:webmaster@sciencentral.com. (2019). Alexander Graham Bell. Pbs.org. https://www.pbs.org/transistor/album1/addlbios/bellag.html

Secoy, D. (n.d.). Grey Owl (Archibald Stansfeld Belaney) – Indigenous Saskatchewan Encyclopedia | University of Saskatchewan. Teaching.usask.ca. https://teaching.usask.ca/indigenoussk/import/grey_owl_archibald_stansfield_belaney.php

Silverman, E. L., & McLeod, S. (2018a). Henrietta Edwards | The Canadian Encyclopedia. Thecanadianencyclopedia.ca. https://www.thecanadianencyclopedia.ca/en/article/henrietta-louise-edwards

Silverman, E. L., & McLeod, S. (2018b). Louise McKinney | The Canadian Encyclopedia. Thecanadianencyclopedia.ca. https://www.thecanadianencyclopedia.ca/en/article/louise-mckinney

Smith, D. B. (2008, June 17). Archibald Belaney, Grey Owl | The Canadian Encyclopedia. Www.thecanadianencyclopedia.ca. https://www.thecanadianencyclopedia.ca/en/article/archibald-belaney-grey-owl

Susan Munroe. (2019). Biography of Nellie McClung, Canadian Activist for Women's Rights. ThoughtCo. https://www.thoughtco.com/nellie-mcclung-508318

The Arctic Expedition of Sir John Franklin (1845 – 1848). (n.d.). Climate in Arts and History. https://www.science.smith.edu/climatelit/the-arctic-expedition-of-sir-john-franklin-1845-1848/

The Nellie McClung Foundation. (n.d.). Nellie McClung | the Nellie McClung Foundation. Nellie McClung. https://www.nelliemcclungfoundation.com/about-nellie

The Story of Mary Macdonald. (n.d.). Villa Les Rochers: Summer Residence of Sir John A. And Lady Agnes Macdonald. https://www.communitystories.ca/v2/les-rochers/story/story-mary-macdonald/

Timeline of Human Rights Development in Canada-Key 9.1.2 a Note: Cut out each event without the date. (n.d.). https://www.edu.gov.mb.ca/k12/cur/socstud/foundation_gr9/blms/9-1-2a.pdf

Tomlinson, A. (2016, February 7). Black History Month: Remembering Canadian civil rights icon Viola Desmond. CBC. https://www.cbc.ca/news/canada/viola-desmond-wanda-robson-black-history-month-1.3430629

Toolkit, W. E. (2015, May 11). Lucy Maud Montgomery and Anne of Green Gables. Www.princeedwardisland.ca. https://www.princeedwardisland.ca/en/information/lucy-maud-montgomery-and-anne-of-green-gables

Twitter. (2014, October 3). Erebus, Lost in 1846 Seeking Northwest Passage, Has Been Found. Los Angeles Times. https://www.latimes.com/world/mexico-americas/la-fg-mexico-americas-canada-shipwreck-20141003-story.html

Valour Canada. (2016, October 7). Byng and Currie | The Road to Vimy Ridge. Vimy Ridge.valour canada.ca. https://vimyridge.valourcanada.ca/the-road-to-vimy-ridge/gearing-up/byng-and-currie/

Viola Desmond – A Brief History of a Nova Scotia Trailblazer. (n.d.). Www.ambassatours.com. https://www.ambassatours.com/post/viola-desmond-a-brief-history

Waite, P. B. (2013, September 22). Confederation | The Canadian Encyclopedia. Thecanadianencyclopedia.ca; The Canadian Encyclopedia. https://www.thecanadianencyclopedia.ca/en/article/confederation

Wayne Gretzky was the Great One from the Start. (2018, June 21). CBC. https://www.cbc.ca/archives/the-young-wayne-gretzky-was-already-the-great-one-1.4684050

Wayne Gretzky. (2023, September 25). Biography. https://www.biography.com/athlete/wayne-gretzky

What Were Residential Schools in Canada? (2021, August 29). Settlement.org. https://settlement.org/ontario/immigration-citizenship/citizenship/first-nations-inuit-and-metis-peoples/what-were-canada-s-residential-schools/

Whitelaw, M. (2023, January 5). How the Inuit Shaped Arctic Exploration. Resources.arctickingdom.com. https://resources.arctickingdom.com/how-the-inuit-shaped-arctic-exploration

Who was Sir Wilfrid Laurier? | Wilfrid Laurier University. (n.d.). Www.wlu.ca. https://www.wlu.ca/about/assets/resources/sir-wilfrid-laurier.html

Who Was Viola Desmond? | Wonderopolis. (n.d.). Wonderopolis.org. https://wonderopolis.org/wonder/Who-Was-Viola-Desmond

Wilfrid Laurier | The Canada Guide. (2016). The Canada Guide. https://thecanadaguide.com/history/prime-ministers/wilfrid-laurier/

Women's Suffrage | The Nellie McClung Foundation. (n.d.). Nellie McClung. https://www.nelliemcclungfoundation.com/womens-suffrage

www.ingramcontent.com/pod-product-compliance
Lightning Source LLC
Chambersburg PA
CBHW071518120626
46550CB00006B/2266